THE
INVISIBLE
ENEMY

Celebrating
30 Years of Publishing
in India

THE INVISIBLE ENEMY

A GLOBAL HISTORY OF CHEMICAL AND BIOLOGICAL WARFARE

GIRISH KUBER

TRANSLATED BY SUBHA PANDE

HarperCollins *Publishers* India

Originally published in Marathi as *Yuddha Jivanche* in 2010
by Rajhans Prakashan

First published in English by HarperCollins *Publishers* 2023
4th Floor, Tower A, Building No. 10, DLF Cyber City,
DLF Phase II, Gurugram, Haryana – 122002
www.harpercollins.co.in

2 4 6 8 10 9 7 5 3 1

P-ISBN: 978-93-5629-690-9
E-ISBN: 978-93-5629-692-3

Typeset in 11/14.2 Adobe Caslon Pro at
Manipal Technologies Limited, Manipal

Printed and bound at
Replika Press Pvt. Ltd, India

This book is produced from independently certified FSC® paper to ensure
responsible forest management.

A tribute to all guinea pigs ... some of them Homo sapiens

Contents

Preface

IT was August 2009. I received a frantic call from a friend who had just moved to London. Even before she could get her life in order there, a mysterious fever gripped her. For the record, it was like any other fever, accompanied by a runny nose and mild headache. There was nothing to be panicky about, especially in London, which is one of the best cities for healthcare.

The panic was a result of developments in India, which was in the grip of a severe spread of the H1N1 flu just when she was leaving Mumbai for London. It was the beginning of the pandemic popularly known as the swine flu. The first few deaths in Pune and Ahmedabad created mass hysteria around this invisible enemy in the twenty-first century. Pune was visibly shaken. Known for their argumentative nature and ever willing to talk down anyone, the virus had Punekars silenced. Two things were in terrible short supply, and to get those, Punekars were seen spending their days and nights in unending serpentine queues—face masks and the tablet Tamiflu. Face masks as a preventive measure and Tamiflu as an SOS.

Such was the frenzy that even the healthier ones were anxious and seen buying and stocking up on Tamiflu.

By the time my friend left for London, the H1N1 influenza had attained devilish proportions and there were very few who were left unimpacted by it or did not consider it an apocalyptic time in India's history. My friend certainly was not one of those. But the nervousness of being alone in a relatively unknown city was enough to scare her into believing that, like hundreds of Indians, she, too, was an H1N1 victim. But unlike hundreds of Indians back home, she was deprived of the luxury of walking into a pharmacy in London and buying Tamiflu, the alleged life saviour then, over the counter. In that part of the world, as we all know, medicines are sold strictly only on a doctor's prescription.

This was the reason she was trying to reach out to me, begging for some Tamiflu tablets to be sent from Mumbai. My panic-stricken friend by then had come to the conclusion that these 'gora' (white) doctors were useless, one of reasons being that her GP (general practitioner) in London had simply refused to prescribe Tamiflu. Instead, he had told her to rest, have piping-hot soups at least twice a day and had given her unassuming paracetamol tablets only to be consumed if the fever climbed over 100 degree Fahrenheit. The National Health Service (NHS) doctor ignored her pleas for Tamiflu. He didn't succumb to her requests for swab testing either. 'Nothing until after a week,' was his only response.

Having spent sleepless nights and days, and adding to her relatives' and friends' consternation back in India, my friend called on the doctor on the seventh day. By then her cold was gone and the fever had disappeared. Free of any of flu-like symptoms, the doctor took a swab to reconfirm his diagnosis.

And voila! All tests were negative. At this point the kind-hearted doctor spoke about how people from the Third World (read India) fell prey to pharmaceutical companies' machinations and, as a result, overmedicate themselves.

It was quite an eye-opener. This made me read up more on pandemics, the alleged role of pharma companies and the doctor–pharma company–establishment nexus.

That was the first seed sown for this book. Around the same time, while reading about the Cold War, I came across various allegations levelled against the US. In one such instance, Cuba's President Fidel Castro had expressed 'profound suspicion' on behalf of fellow citizens that a series of disastrous crop blights and dengue epidemic, which had killed 113 people, including 81 children, had been deliberately introduced into Cuba. The report in the *New York Times* had pointed a finger at the Central Intelligence Agency—the omnipresent CIA.

Thus began my quest to learn more about the topic, which resulted in me acquiring more than half a dozen books on chemical/biological warfare and pharma companies' misadventures. There were many reference points. *Roche versus Adams* by Stanley Adams was the first book on the pharma industry that came to mind, which I had read in my school days. I also remembered the thalidomide tragedy, exposed by Harold Evans in *The Sunday Times*, London. Evans later became the editor of *The Sunday Times*. In the 1950s and 1960s, thalidomide was a commonly used drug for the treatment of nausea in pregnant women. However, it came to light later that thalidomide treatment resulted in severe birth defects in thousands of children. Evans's journalism played a key role in exposing this dark truth. His book *Good Times, Bad Times*, which chronicles *The Times*' journalism and journey, is one of my all-time favourites.

As I kept reading on the topic, the urge to tell this story to the world became stronger. Eventually it resulted in a book, *Yuddha Jivanche*, first published in Marathi in 2010.

Usually twelve years is enough to send any book into oblivion. But this one proved to be an exception. Around a decade after it was first published, demand for this book saw an exponential growth, thanks to yet another avatar of the invisible enemy. Scientists and researchers named it the SARS-CoV-2 virus. For the layman it was simply Covid, a severely virulent mutation of the old H1N1. Even after millions of death worldwide and a global vaccination drive to prevent its spread, the SARS-CoV-2 virus simply refuses to vanish.

Also refusing to vanish is the debate over the origins of this virus. There have been hundreds of reports and an equal, if not more, number of explanations about Covid's genesis. But the more important question is: Was this virus an accident or was it 'designed'? In case of the latter, who could be behind its spread? A number of theories are doing the rounds—and the most popular revolves around a laboratory in Wuhan, the capital of Hubei Province in China. Thanks to this virus, the way we live our lives has been drastically altered—and it will take a long time before our lives go back to pre-Covid days. The scars this virus has left on us will also take a while to heal. Moreover, no one knows whether the truth about the virus will ever come out. Even if it does, it doesn't seem to be happening any time soon.

But when the present and the future both look uncertain, it's time to look at the past. That's exactly what this book is about. It's a story about how faceless viruses and odourless chemicals were used— many times knowingly—for the most heinous things human beings can ever do. Along the way it also talks about how the art of killing people has evolved over the years.

And the process is still on.

The Germs Are at Peace

THE Gilead Sciences office in California bore a festive look. After being down for a while, the pharmaceutical company was showing signs of recovery and getting into shape. Its share price, which had been tumbling under the force of gravity in the New York share market, was after a long time holding its own. The company's fortunes had clearly turned, and it was in for good times. The management and employees were elated and looked forward to healthy bonuses after a wait of five years.

Gilead Sciences had US President George W. Bush to thank for this turnaround. He had realized he needed to show he cared for the health of his people—just enough to be seen as a benevolent President. However, as he was the supreme leader of the world's sole superpower, it wouldn't have looked proper if he only appeared to be looking after the welfare of US citizens. He had to be seen as caring for humanity as a whole. It was a mindset he had inherited from his father, George H.W. Bush.

What did the compassionate President actually do towards this end? He made a massive allocation of funds towards healthcare, headlined by a visit to the National Institutes of Health offices in Bethesda, Maryland, on 1 November 2005, where he delivered an impassioned speech on the worrisome future of healthcare across the world. President Bush claimed to be so concerned about a potential healthcare crisis that he even invited the director of the World Health Organization (WHO) to Bethesda. Members of his cabinet were also present, and Secretary of State Condoleezza Rice.

In his speech, President Bush announced the most ambitious healthcare reform programme of all time, under which he gave himself the right to spend $7.1 billion. He could consequently allocate the money as he pleased, without the assent of the United States of America's senate or Congress. He was not even duty-bound to provide any accounts of expenditure. The all-encompassing programme covered the entire world's health issues. It had details about the threat of diseases faced by various countries, along with measures for prevention and cure, and nutritional and dietary requirements to build immunity.

Gilead Sciences had to be indebted to President Bush, for, thanks to his speech and its focus on universal healthcare, demand for the company's unique product rose astronomically worldwide. The reason was simple: no other company was manufacturing that product. It was the only available treatment for a particular disease. The only company making the medicine was in the US. Seemingly a simple coincidence and a matter of chance.

In yet another coincidence, a minister from George Bush Sr's time was a former chairman of the company. The company and the minister's fortunes rose simultaneously.

Such coincidences are quite common. It's just that ordinary people like you and I cannot see them for what they are.

The disease was bird flu.

The drug was Tamiflu.

And the person who took the most advantage and garnered the most profits was a prominent US politician.[1]

This raises a few questions.

What is the connection between a pharmaceutical company, its former chairman who happened to be in the US cabinet, the US President's huge healthcare package, and the spread of bird flu? The prospect of a bird flu outbreak sent people all over the world into a panic, but, as reports emerged then, it turned out to be very good news for Defence Secretary Donald Rumsfeld and other politically connected investors in Gilead Sciences.

Rumsfeld served as Gilead's chairman from 1997 until 2001, when he joined the Bush administration. He owned a stake in Gilead valued at between $5 million and $25 million, according to federal financial disclosures filed by him. Soon, fears of a pandemic and the demand for Tamiflu sent Gilead's stock value up to $47 from $35. That made the Pentagon chief—already one of the wealthiest members of the Bush cabinet—at least $1 million richer.

---

1   *New York Times*, 'Rumsfeld to Avoid Bird-Flu Drug Issues', 28 October 2005.
     'Defense Secretary Donald H. Rumsfeld has recused himself from government decisions concerning medications to prevent or treat avian flu, rather than sell his stock holdings in the company that patented the antiviral agent Tamiflu, according to a Pentagon memorandum issued Thursday. The memorandum, to Mr Rumsfeld's staff from the Pentagon general counsel, said the defense secretary would not take part in decisions that may affect his financial interests in Gilead Sciences Inc. Before becoming defense secretary in January 2001, Mr Rumsfeld was chairman of Gilead. On each of his annual financial disclosure statements, he has listed continued stock holdings in the company. Gilead holds the patent on Tamiflu, but contracts for it are signed with an American subsidiary of F. Hoffman-LaRoche Ltd, which holds marketing and manufacturing rights. Mr Rumsfeld will remain involved in matters related to the Pentagon response to an outbreak, so long as none affect Gilead.'

Interestingly, Rumsfeld isn't the only political heavyweight benefiting from the demand for Tamiflu, which is now manufactured and marketed by Swiss pharma giant Roche. (Gilead receives a royalty from Roche equalling about 10 per cent of sales.) Former US Secretary of State George Shultz, who is on Gilead's board, has sold more than $7 million worth of Gilead shares since the beginning of 2005.

What about the outbreak of swine flu that followed bird flu? And what about the other epidemics that have taken place over the years, such as plague, amoebiasis and anthrax, killing lakhs of people in poor and underdeveloped countries?

This is the story of biological warfare—and the chemical assassins behind it.

1

The Immortal Game of Killing Mortals

THE evolutionary history of mankind sometimes reads like a handbook of innovative ways to annihilate human life. That is, while man has over the ages constantly strived to evolve in a civilized society, reach dizzying heights in science and develop modern medicines to defeat death, he has, at the same time, been trying to find novel ways of killing fellow humans. This paradox can be seen imprinted clearly at every stage in history and folklore, reflected in epic mythological works like the Mahabharata, ancient Greek writings, Renaissance Europe and the actions of present-day superpowers such as Russia and the US. The practice of killing humans is timeless.

Several disciplines and subjects were at the mercy of this effort in the Western world, while India and other Third World countries contributed in the capacity of experimental labs and guinea pigs, given the first chance to be victims of any new killer development.

The results of these experiments were studied in depth. It can also be said that history has endorsed such developments.

Even in ancient times, people were falling victim to what we today call chemical warfare. Knowledge about chemical warfare existed during the Babylonian civilization; however, the chemicals in question were not developed in labs, but derived from natural sources like leaves, bark, flowers and mineral ores.[2] As far back as 3000 BCE, there is a mention of hydrocyanic acid being used in Egypt.[3] Smoke screens of poisonous gases and soporific medicines being sprayed in the air was a common occurrence. The systematic method of producing poisonous gases to be used in war is clearly mentioned in Chinese manuscripts from 1000 BCE.

In the seventh century, between 638 BCE and 559 BCE, the Assyrians—hailing from parts of present-day Egypt and Syria— would add poisonous chemicals to the water bodies of enemy kingdoms. During the Solon war in the same period, they secretly fed enemy soldiers strong purgatives and killed them once they became weak with severe diarrhoea. There are records of water bodies being poisoned with harmful chemicals during the war between Athens and Sicyon in 590 BCE, causing severe diarrhoea among the Sicyon people and enabling the Greeks to win.

Later, in 428 BCE, during the Spartan war, chemical weapons were used in a manner which strikes one as familiar today. A mixture of wild fruit extracts and arsenic was poured over the boundary walls of enemy towns and set afire. Thousands died inhaling the poisonous smoke. According to historical records, similar methods were used in China during the same period to kill enemies.

---

2   Thomas J. Johnson, *A History of Biological Warfare from 300 BCE to the Present*, pp. 1–5.

3   C. Hilmas, Jeffrey Smart and Benjamin Hill, *History of Chemical Warfare*, Chapter 2, pp, 1–3.

There were further advancements in the field during the reign of the Roman Empire. In the period between 82 BCE and 78 BCE, the Romans successfully developed poisonous gases which could cause blindness, helping them win several wars. Later, the Christians used the same gases to stop the aggressive Turkish warriors. Arsenic was used in these gases as well. The Austrian historian Von Senftenberg wrote: 'The evil Christians should never use such dangerous weapons against other Christians. It's alright that these were used against the Turks, but they must be careful not to use them against our Christian brethren.'

In the Byzantine era, this field evolved further. The Greeks developed chemicals which they spread on ocean waters and set fire to, along with natural volatile and inflammable materials, causing enemy boats to perish within minutes. In Constantinople, present-day Istanbul, Kallinikos had mastery over this form of warfare. Kallinikos, also spelled 'Callinicus' (AD 673), was a well-known architect of the era, and is credited with the invention of Greek fire—a highly incendiary liquid that was projected from 'siphons' to enemy ships or troops and was almost impossible to extinguish. Born in Syria, Kallinikos was a Jewish refugee who was forced to flee the Arabs to Constantinople. With this, the Greeks could ignite any kind of water. In the Constantinople war of 677 BCE, they used this technique to break the siege of the Muslims. Such new techniques of warfare were also used in the Renaissance period in Europe. Leonardo Da Vinci, creator of the famed Mona Lisa work of art, made cannon balls composed of a mixture of sulphur, copper acetate and arsenic. Once these exploded, the poisonous fumes destroyed human lungs.

Apart from being skilled in using poisonous chemicals, our ancestors were masters in biological warfare as well. It is mentioned in *Philoctetes*, a play staged by Sophocles in 400 BCE. The protagonist, Philoctetes, gets wounded by a poisonous arrow during the Trojan war. This war is a part of Greek mythology and is culturally as important as the Mahabharata for India. It finds ample mention in Greek and Roman literature and is part of several classics like *The Iliad* and *The Odyssey* by Homer. The plot is complex, based on the fight among the Greek gods Athena, Hera and Aphrodite, as a result of which Helen, the beautiful wife of the Spartan King Menelaus, is abducted by Paris, the Trojan prince. Paris had entered King Menelaus's palace in the guise of a political advisor; at the same moment, Helen was injured by the love arrow of the god of beauty, Eros, causing her to fall in love with Paris. He abducts her and brings her to Troy, leading to the Trojan war, somewhere between the eleventh and thirteenth centuries.[4]

The point to note is that the Trojan war too can be said to be a case of biological warfare, though mythologized. Not only do mentions of this war cite biological weapons, they also contain the origin of the term. The word 'toxin' or 'poison' comes from the root Greek word 'toxicon', derived from 'toxon', meaning arrow in Greek. Reading descriptions of how ancient Greek warriors infused their arrows with poison causes goose bumps even today. Armies would add human blood and dung to carcasses of poisonous animals. The mixture would then be kept in pots and allowed to decay for several days. A large number of arrows would be kept dipped into that poisonous mix for months before they were ready to be used in war. How many arrows could be shot at a time? As per historical records, a strong Greek soldier could hit a target 1600 feet away by releasing twenty poisonous arrows in a minute. This gives us an idea how mighty their armies would have been. Even if a victim of a poisonous arrow wasn't beheaded, he surely wouldn't survive because the poison had two lethal effects: gangrene and lockjaw. In some cases, people were known to die of severe respiratory problems.

---

4   Robert Graves, *The Greek Myths: The Complete and Definitive Edition.*

In the Polynesian war, the Spartans attacked the city of Athens, causing widespread carnage by poisoning wells, killing thousands of civilians. This battle which took place between 431 BCE and 404 BCE has been written about in several Greek texts of the time. At the same time, Athens was struck by the plague, leading to the belief that there was a connection between the two events. It would have been a surprise if the Spartans hadn't won the war after the use of such cruel and heinous methods. They were criticized widely for it and the use of bioweapons retreated into the background.

But the reprieve was short-lived and such methods of warfare soon made a comeback. In the battle of Pergamon that began in 241 BCE, for instance, the Carthaginian general Hannibal carried mud pots filled with poisonous snakes. When the Pergamon boats came to stop him, he and his army threw these pots at them. The snakes proved to be his secret weapon and he won the battle.

Everything is considered fair in war. But such harsh means to gain victory started becoming common in normal civilian life as well. At the beginning of the Christian era, a very cruel way of punishing a sinner was devised. He would be tied to the carcass of a person who had died of a dangerous disease. Gradually, the sinner too would get affected by the same disease and begin withering away inch by inch. The worst part was that the kin of the sinner would be informed that he had died, thus leaving him without any solace as he neared the end.

But the Tartar armies took this thinking to the limit during the Mongol period in the 1300s in Caffa, a city in present-day Ukraine. They used the cadavers of those who had died of disease as weapons. Using a long sling shot or catapult, they would fling the dead body on to enemy soldiers, the contact causing them to contract plague-like diseases. Sometimes human carcasses would be replaced with dead rats. The intent behind both approaches was the same: to spread disease.

The Tartars achieved great victories this way. The Tartar–Mongol war lasted for three years, from 1347 to 1350, and the dead bodies spread the plague far and wide. During that time, a few Italians were visiting the area for trade, and by the time they realized what was happening, it was too late. Some of them contracted the plague and the Tartar rats also found their way into their boats. The twin curses of plague-ridden rats and humans left footprints of the disease everywhere they landed in Europe, where its spread was recorded by several historians. It reached Italy, France and Spain, and within a year, the Scandinavian countries. It terrorized Paris, London, Oxford and other cities. It caused severe havoc in England, with almost 66 per cent of Londoners falling prey to the disease. The plague killed almost 1.5 crore people in Europe. The epidemic had become so serious that its tremors were felt several times for the next 400 years.

Different people looked at the epidemic differently. Some felt it was a divine curse while others believed it was atonement for human sins. Some even disfigured themselves as a means of penitence. They believed that if they caused trauma to themselves, the plague would stay away. They would burn the lumps caused by the disease in their armpits with heated iron rods. The medical science department of the University of Paris recorded the seriousness of the plague epidemic. In the year 1345, the university said that the planetary positions around Earth had changed and the plague was a consequence of that. If an educational institution believed in such things, what could be said of the common man! These beliefs only strengthened and gave a fillip to priests and clerics who happily washed their white cassocks and robes in this divine occurrence. Some Catholic priests blamed the sins of Jews for the plague. This belief spread like wildfire and led to the killing of Jews in large numbers across Europe.

The whole of Europe was battered by the plague and industries went bust. There was no labour available for work and universities were emptied of both students and teachers. Nobody had a clue about what was happening. That time came to be called the 'black period' in history.

There are three types of the disease. In the bubonic plague, pus-filled lumps grow in the armpits and thighs and the patient develops fever. Eventually, the lumps burst and the patient dies. At that time, 75 per cent of bubonic plague patients did not survive. The second type was the pneumonic plague, in which the lungs of the patient fill with fluid and they die of a severe cough where blood is expelled (hemoptysis). About 90–95 per cent of people afflicted by pneumonic plague died. The third and most lethal form of plague was the black plague, in which the mortality rate was 100 per cent. The disease-causing bacteria attack the circulatory system; the patient's blood turns purple and the skin blue-black, and a high fever breaks out. There is no cure to this date.

The biggest problem at the time was the unwillingness of doctors to treat plague-affected patients. The moment people came to know that someone had been afflicted by the black plague, everyone, including family members, would isolate the patient and leave him or her to die alone. If a patient discovered they had a lump in the armpit, they would voluntarily inform everyone of the illness and go out of town and live in isolation, waiting to die. Once the afflicted person died, people refused to go anywhere near the body. Hence, bodies would lie strewn all over the streets, waiting to be devoured by vultures and other scavengers. These details are gory even to read; it is difficult to imagine how it would have been to experience such things at the time. Europe suffered from this killer disease for generations—all caused by an insignificant war!

Details have been found of Napoleon Bonaparte using similar methods 300 years later against the Italians. In the battle of 1797, known as the Battle of Rivoli, when Napoleon's ships were docked at the Italian port, attempts were made to spread fever-causing microbes. Enough has been written about how fever played an important role in Napoleon's victory over the British in the battle of Walcheren in 1809. This was the largest British expedition of that year, however, it failed to achieve any of its goals, thanks to 'Walcheren Fever'. Within a month of seizing the island, the British troops had over 8,000 fever cases. Although more than 4,000 British troops died during the expedition, only 106 died in combat; the survivors withdrew on 9 December.

At the age of eighteen, the legendary saint, Joan of Arc, claimed to have had visions in which god had told her to save France by expelling its enemies and installing Charles VII as its rightful king. She commanded the French army and won several wars against England, eventually being captured during the battle at Burgundy, where the locals sold her to the English establishment. A church trial pronounced her guilty and she was burnt at the stake as a nineteen-year-old. She was not idolized initially, but 500 years later, the Vatican accepted her greatness and granted her sainthood in 1920. She is now revered as a national saint in France.[5]

Even with the involvement of priests and religious heads, there was no end to the gruesome biological warfare of those times. Dead animals and decaying human body parts or whole human cadavers were used like bombs, with the sole intention being to spread contagious diseases among enemy forces. In the war between Russia and Sweden in 1710, such diseased bodies are known to have been used in and around Estonia. Though there were some signs of humanity in the North American war between 1747 and 1767, it wasn't as if the deliberate attempt at spreading diseases had stopped.

Sir Jeffrey Amherst (1717–97) was the commander of the British forces in North America, where they had brought the indigenous Red Indians to their knees. Amherst sought permission from the British government to reduce the population of the Red Indians. A smallpox

---

5   'St. Joan of Arc', *Catholic Encyclopedia*.

epidemic had spread in that region and some British soldiers caught the infection. Though they were getting treatment for the disease, the rashes took time to dry and would develop pus and burst. The patients needed a lot of care as the environment did not allow the rashes to dry fast. Seeing the plight of his own soldiers, a captain in Sir Amherst's platoon, Captain Fauquier, got an idea. He started storing the handkerchiefs, blankets and other personal clothing of his sick soldiers without washing them. Normally, these were burnt to prevent spread of the disease. Once he had accumulated a large number of these items, he invited the Red Indians to his camp in the name of some ceremony. They could not see through the trickery of the British, and when Amherst and Fauquier offered the infected handkerchiefs and blankets to them as gifts, they did not decline. To add insult to the intended injury they were told, 'You will get the expected results of these loving gifts and I am sure you will pay heed to them.' Their captain made a note of the day's events in his diary. 'I am sure; we will get the desired results.' And he was proven right.

In what is present-day Ohio, thousands thus died of the smallpox epidemic, and it soon spread all over the US. It had not existed there before then. This was the first time in history that locals died due to a disease that was brought in from outside the continent.

Like a silver lining among the dark clouds, Edward Jenner proved to be the divine light amidst the epidemic. We must acknowledge his achievements in this area.

Jenner was born on 17 May 1749 in Berkeley, Gloucestershire, England. His father was a clergyman while his mother was a small-time traditional medic who treated the villagers' simple diseases with her home remedies. The young boy was curious about nature and the functioning of the human mind and body. He found his formal education inadequate to quell his curiosity, and that led him to work as an apprentice for the village doctor, Daniel Ludlow, at the tender age of fourteen. Following an eight-year stint with Dr Ludlow, he joined St. George's Hospital in London in 1770 and started learning human anatomy and surgery from the reputed surgeon Dr John Hunter. Jenner developed mastery over several subjects and could speak confidently on different topics like the human body, birds and trees. He also wrote occasionally.

Gloucestershire was hit by a small-pox epidemic in 1788. Amidst the panic, Jenner noticed that the milkman who delivered milk to his house appeared oddly calm. This surprised him and one day he decided to find out the reason. The milkman couldn't explain anything and just said, 'We milkmen and dairy maids don't get infected with smallpox.' Not convinced with his explanation, Jenner went to the milkman's house to check the conditions he lived in, and his cowshed. He couldn't figure out the reason, but as it turned out, he was on the right path. He realized that the cows had been afflicted with smallpox too—with the disease manifesting with boils, rashes and pus; just like in humans. It was cow pox. Jenner surmised that since the milkmen had been in contact with the cows, their bodies had developed resistance to it.

But for his theory to be proved, the microbes causing the disease had to be injected into someone's body. Who would possibly volunteer for that? Jenner couldn't find a single person. After a lot of struggle, an opportunity presented itself on 14 May 1796. He found a young dairy maid, Sarah Nelms, who had fresh cowpox lesions on her hands and arms. Using matter from Nelms's lesions, he inoculated eight-year-old James Phipps. He made a sharp cut on Phipps's leg, and once it started bleeding, filled the cut with the pus and matter collected from Nelms's body and bandaged it. Jenner asked the farmers to take care of the boy and told them to keep him informed about the boy's condition.

Phipps came to Jenner within two days to say that he was feeling weak. Jenner was actually relieved—this was as per his expectations.

Over the next two days, Phipps lost his sense of taste and got even weaker. But these symptoms subsided within two days and then his condition improved.

Jenner's experiment had now reached an important stage. He had to introduce the smallpox organisms into Phipps's body. He explained the procedure to him, saying, 'If this experiment succeeds, then not just you, but all of humanity will be free from smallpox.' The boy asked, 'What if it fails?' Jenner said calmly, 'I will be convicted for murder.' Despite what he heard, Phipps did not back out. In a month's time, Jenner inoculated the boy's body with the material he collected from a smallpox patient. His father and Jenner watched Phipps like a hawk. When he developed fever within two days, the rashes appeared. Jenner was now worried.

But the rashes did not change into smallpox. This convinced Jenner that a vaccine for smallpox was possible. He sent the results of his experiment to the Royal Society of London. But they did not pay attention to his findings. Jenner continued with his experiments, nevertheless. He performed the same procedure on twenty-three other people and got similar results. He continued to inform the Royal Society about his findings, but when he got no response, decided to publish his work on his own.

The word for cow in Latin is *vacca*, and the cowpox disease was called *vaccina*. Jenner combined the two words and coined the word *vaccin*. This is how what we know today as 'vaccine' came into being. In time, not only the Royal Society but the British Parliament too acknowledged his work and asked Jenner to continue his experiments. They offered him a grant of 30,000 pounds in two instalments.

Jenner spent his entire life working on vaccines. He didn't earn much, but became famous the world over. He built a house and a small cottage in his courtyard and named it 'House of Vaccine'. The Lancet, in 2011, wrote, '... the Chantry, a handsome Queen Anne house just over the wall from Berkeley Castle, is the place where world history really was made. The Chantry was the residence of Edward Jenner (1749–1823), doctor and polymath, for the last half of his life. This is where Jenner undertook and wrote up his experiments, while running a single-handed medical practice that covered almost 400 square miles; it was also the family home where he lived a full life, raised his children, watched his wife and son succumb to tuberculosis, and died. The world knows this as the place where, on 14 May 1796, Jenner did the first properly recorded vaccination, on his gardener's 8-year-old son.' He gave free vaccinations to poor people. His technique spread worldwide and throughout Europe, and people began injecting themselves with disease-causing organisms. In 1800, Jenner gave the details of all his experiments and a sample of the smallpox vaccine to his friend Dr Benjamin Waterhouse, a professor of physics at Harvard University. He tried Jenner's method in his own region of New England in the US. The vaccine worked and Dr Waterhouse was able to save his entire family from the smallpox epidemic in the area. Once Dr Waterhouse was certain of the vaccine's efficacy, he met Thomas Jefferson (who became US President in 1801 and laid the foundation for democracy with the Declaration of Independence). Jefferson had a scientific bent of mind and could appreciate the logic of Jenner's technique. He unhesitatingly tried the experiment on his whole family, including children.

The experiment worked, and the visionary leader wrote an emotional letter to Edward Jenner, 'Smallpox was an incurable disease and your efforts made us conquer the disease. Generations to come will be indebted to you forever!'

Jefferson's words were proven true, and two centuries later, smallpox was completely eradicated from the face of Earth. But Jenner was not alive to see this happen. He had suffered a stroke which paralysed the right side of his body, leading to his death on

23 January 1823. But death had already been his constant companion for thirteen years before his own demise.[6]

Jenner's oldest son, Edward, had died of tuberculosis in 1810, and his sister, Mary, the same year. Two years later, his younger sister, Anne, and in 1815, his wife, Catherine, too died of the same illness. Jenner was devastated and lost the will to live himself. He withdrew completely from public life.

But he had laid the foundation for vaccinations at a time when the fields of immunology and microbiology didn't even exist, barring a few similar experiments that had been tried before his time. The technique of injecting disease-causing organisms into human bodies existed in India, China and the Ottoman Empire, where the women chosen to be in the emperor's harem had to be inoculated before being allowed in. In 1715, Lady Mary Wortley Montague, wife of the British ambassador to Turkey, got to know of this method and created a sensation by getting herself inoculated with smallpox micro-organisms. She was so convinced that she even got her five-year-old son, Edward, inoculated once she returned to England. But the credit for developing the method in a scientific manner went to Edward Jenner. 'It was a daring and dangerous experiment that paved the way for the development of the first safe vaccine and saved countless lives. Yet, when Lady Mary Wortley Montagu deliberately infected her own daughter with a tiny dose of smallpox—successfully inoculating the three-year-old child in 1721—her ideas were dismissed and she was denounced by eighteenth-century society as an "ignorant woman". If she had not inoculated her daughter, we would not then have gone on ultimately to find a cure for smallpox,' writes Jo Willett, author of *The Pioneering Life of Mary Wortley Montagu*,

---

6   Edward Jenner (1749–1823), http://www.bbc.co.uk/history/historic-figures/jenner-edward.shtml; Stefan Riedel, 'Edward Jenner and the History of Smallpox and Vaccination', Proceedings (Baylor University. Medical Center), 2005.

published in 2021. Later Jenner was felicitated for his monumental work by the British government and a museum was established in his name. His statue was erected at Trafalgar Square, later moved to the prestigious Kensington Gardens. It still stands there, but is not noticed because people are more interested in searching for signs and symbols of present-day royalty. Most people don't even think of the reason behind the large, round vaccination marks on their upper arms given to them as infants. Now there is no need to either. Smallpox has disappeared forever.

This was Edward Jenner's achievement. It laid the foundation for the impending fight against fatal diseases and the study of immunology.

2

Just for a Single Breath

YPRES, one among the many idyllic towns in Belgium, produced an abundance of dairy products like milk and butter that brought prosperity to the area. The only sin the town committed was to come in the way of Germany's invasion of France during the First World War.

The war had just started and Germany's ambitions and future plans were becoming quite clear. One evening, the shelling had died down at around 5 p.m., and the French military division, Algerian reserve forces and Allied Canadian soldiers were resting while a cool evening breeze wafted around. The German camp too was enjoying its break. But the reverie of the Allied forces was broken as they realized a strange smell was spreading around them. Soon, a greenish-yellow cloud was floating over the camp. The Allied soldiers soon found it difficult to breathe, their faces getting contorted as if they were being strangled. They became desperate for a single breath; some writhed around, while others coughed. Breathing was becoming impossible. Some started walking towards their trenches, but were trapped further because the greenish-yellow cloud had descended to the level of their knees. There was no breeze that could dissipate it. It had reached inside the trenches. Those who had gone in there were stuck like insects in a spider's web. Many were now spitting blood, while others frothed green foam at their mouths. A deathly silence was all around. The game was over!

This, in fact, was the first recorded attack using chemicals and it took the lives of 6,500 soldiers.[7] They had no chance of escape; what would they have escaped from? Never before had invisible messengers of death arrived airborne. The soldiers didn't know whom to fight when the air itself became a foe! On the opposite side, the Germans were keeping a keen eye on developments. They had hauled heavy metallic cylinders and released the poisonous gas into the air—5,730 cylinders had been kept ready over an area of 6.5 km. They took care to release the gas in small batches in the direction of the evening breeze. The cylinders contained 168 tons of chlorine that had been sourced from BASF, Hoechst and Bayer to kill human beings. If chlorine is inhaled in small quantities it is not fatal, but in large quantities it affects the nose, wind pipe, lungs and the mucosal lining. The lungs are irreversibly damaged and fill up with fluid, leading to death due to asphyxiation.

The town gates of Ypres were filled with bodies. Even weapons were damaged by the gas. The canons and guns looked rusted, as if they had been lying wet in the rain for five to ten years. The buttons on the dead soldiers' uniforms had turned blue-black.

Seeing the results of the first chemical war, not only were the Allied countries stunned, but the Germans too were shocked! They hadn't imagined that the attack would have such serious consequences. It had breached nearly 6.5 km of the Allied defence

7   Robert Harris and Jeremy Paxman, *A Higher Form of Killing: The Secret History of Chemical and Biological Warfare*, pp. 3–7.

formation, but even then the Germans did not have enough soldiers to break into the Allied camp. German Commander Falkenhayn was completely taken aback. His experience with chemical warfare had been restricted to the laboratory till then. The realization of the destruction caused did not stop them from using such methods again.

On 24 April 1914 at 2.45 a.m., a wave of the chemical gas was released. This was thirty-six hours after the first attack. Captain Bertram of the Eighth Canadian battalion had just completed preparations for the next day and was going to bed when he got a strange whiff. Suspicious of foul play, he ran out of his tent, but by then the greenish-yellow cloud had reached the barricades. The soldiers began running helter-skelter, causing further damage, as they couldn't breathe while running.

Chlorine gas floats about six feet above the ground and makes breathing extremely difficult. There is no way to escape it at ground level. One could possibly go to a higher level, but since they didn't know what kind of gas it was, they had no clue about how to fight it. Someone suggested placing wet handkerchiefs over noses, but where could they have got water from? Some soldiers urinated into handkerchiefs and tied them on their faces. They felt that the urea in the urine might neutralize the chlorine, but the gas was so dense that the idea failed.

Almost 5,000 Canadian soldiers, including the battalion head, Sergeant Grindlay, lost their lives. Sergeant Grindlay was admitted to the army hospital, but the doctors had no idea what the gas was and how to treat its effects. They conducted an autopsy on his body, hoping that the information could be useful to treat other victims.

'The unidentified gas has discoloured Grindlay's skin colour completely. It has turned blue-black. The lungs have become heavy because of fluid retention. The fluid has a green froth and is sticky. The liquid has turned dense because of contact with air. It is as thick as egg albumin. The wind pipe and all the veins going from the heart to the brain are blocked. Cause of death: lack of air/oxygen.'

The saddest part was that the Allies had been forewarned. A week before the first chemical attack, on 13 April, a French patrol had captured a German soldier carrying an aspirator. Masks and aspirators were a rarity those days. The twenty-four-year-old German private, August Jager of the 26th battalion, was interrogated hard and he sang like a parrot. He revealed that the Germans were planning a chemical gas attack; he also described the positions of the cylinders. This information was passed on to French Divisional Commander General Ferry, who in turn passed it on to the British high command, saying, 'If we have to survive this chemical gas attack, we have to move our soldiers away from that area. Alternatively, we have to give permission to our forces to attack and take control of the gas cylinders. Otherwise, we will have to face serious consequences.'

But nobody did anything. The British military closed General Ferry's file, labelling it 'secret and confidential'. The French sat on the information. Later, when things happened exactly the way General Ferry had predicted, he was dismissed from service, citing inaction. It was the general who had forewarned his seniors about the attack, but his documents revealed the incompetence of the senior officers. Later, he wrote a tell-all book in 1930 that exposed them. The general was perhaps ignorant of the social norm that one shouldn't wash the seniors' dirty linen in public. After the war, the young German private, Jager, was arrested and sentenced with penal servitude for ten years in his home country. The German government filed a case against him in the Leipzig military court and he was convicted for having revealed military secrets and told that his betrayal had caused Germany to lose the war!

The important point to note is that none of the people responsible for using such barbaric methods and causing large-scale manslaughter were ever punished. The people who were the actual culprits walked free while the ones who brought the crime to light were convicted.

At the beginning of the twentieth century, a pact had been signed by several nations regarding the kind of weapons that could be used in war. A convention was held at The Hague, Netherlands, on 18 May 1899 to address this issue. Russia's erstwhile foreign minister, Mikhail Nikolayevich, was instrumental in organizing it. Andrew White was the president of the US delegation.

At that time, new types of bullets were being produced which would form a balloon inside the victim's body and make them impossible to remove, even by surgery. The Hague convention was organized to ban the use of such bullets and go over other aspects of wartime conduct. It prohibited the use of bombs or projectiles that diffused poisonous gases. These discussions went on for almost three and a half months because the nations which had to be convinced were the ones producing these weapons. The discussions ended in a stalemate.

Finally, an agreement was reached on 29 July 1899, and the treaty was signed by all participating nations. It came into force a year later, from 4 September 1900. What Germany did in the First World War was a clear breach of the treaty and a human rights crime. When it was asked for an explanation, the answer was vague and odd.

'We have not breached any treaty. The treaty states that chemical bombs should not be used and chemical weapons should not be fired. We have not done anything like that. We have not used chemical bombs or used projectiles. We had only opened the valves of poisonous gas cylinders. There is no breach of treaty by opening the cylinders by looking at the direction of the wind. Whatever we have done is completely within the rules of war.'

Several German newspapers came to the support of their government. It was clear that it had the support of its people in this dastardly act. This was the scariest aspect of the entire episode.

Britain was shaken after the chemical attack. The British commander at Ypres, John French, asked his government for permission to retaliate. French was a British naval officer from 1866 to 1874, after which he transferred to the army. He played a vital role in Sudan and later in the Boer war (1899–1902). He was promoted to field marshal in 1913 as an appreciation for his invaluable service.

At the beginning of the First World War, he was given commandership of the special British Expeditionary Force (BEF). But the role did not appeal to him, and with the advent of chemical warfare, he was keener on ensuring the safety of his soldiers. That is why he felt that even Britain should possess such weapons. He asked permission from the British government for the same but the war minister, Lord Kitchener, replied, 'Before we fall to the degraded level of the Germans, I must submit the matter to the government.' This meant that if the Germans had fallen one level, Britain was ready to answer them in their own coin by falling two steps down, ready to turn a blind eye to the treaty if need be. The problem was that Britain didn't possess a flourishing chemical industry like Germany, which had chemical giants like BASF, Hoechst and Bayer. At that time, eight massive German chemical companies were bunched together to form a colossal conglomerate called Interessen-Gemeinschaft (IG) with a combined worth of $400 million! At the start of the First World War, Germany held a monopoly over the global chemical industry. Each IG company was so huge that not only Britain, but even the Allied countries together couldn't match up to them. All these companies were in touch with the German government with some of their chemists being war consultants. That is why when a poisonous gas was produced in any of their labs, it was promptly tested in the battlefield. One such experiment was conducted on the Russian border in January 1915. This gas wasn't very poisonous, but once inhaled, it led to eye irritation and tears. It was called 'tear gas' and was a precursor of the 'riot gas' used to disperse rioters and protestors today. It was called 'T-Stoff' at that time, after its inventor, Prof. Hans Tappen, the head of the Kaiser Wilhelm Institute of Physical Chemistry. The tear gas he invented had two parts. The inner part of the shell contained xylyl bromide, separated from the outer casing by a glass container. It became possible to lob these seven pound shells from canons over long distances. As a dedication to his contribution, these shells were named 'T-Stoff'.

But funnily enough, tear gas was first used by the French! Only they didn't call it by that name. In August 1914, the French army had thrown tear gas grenades containing ethyl bromoacetate on the Germans. The only effect they had on the German soldiers was causing them to sneeze. Even the best marksman cannot aim at his target properly while he is suffering a bout of sneezing. The Germans called this chemical '*ni shrapnel*' which is derived from the German word for sneezing powder, '*niespulver*'. These chemicals had no other serious effects. The French stopped getting adequate supplies of ethyl bromoacetate, and then used chloroacetate to create these shells, which didn't prove effective and went unnoticed. Germany used 18,000 xylyl bromide cylinders against Russia on 31 January 1915, in the west of Warsaw during the battle of Bolimov. Instead of vaporizing, the chemical froze, completely failing to have an impact.

The founding father of IG, Carl Duisberg, was disappointed that these gases only dispersed enemy formations but didn't kill them.[8] Duisberg was originally Prussian, and was worse than Hitler when

---

8   Ibid., p. 11: 'The introduction of chemical warfare was in fact actively canvassed by the IG cartel from the outset of the war, most notably by its head Carl Duisberg ... The chemical industry was the foundation of Germany's war machine. Without Duisberg's factories' discovery and mass production of synthetic nitrates, the kaiser would have been forced to sue for peace in 1915 ... [He] urged the employment of chemical warfare at a special conference of the German high command ... later he arranged for the offices of his own company, Bayer, to be decorated with a giant frieze depicting various aspects of

it came to destruction. He strongly believed that Germany should have all the deadliest possible weapons that could annihilate the enemy, and no one ever dared to oppose this powerful industrialist. He would openly say that there was nothing wrong in using any kind of means to develop war capabilities. Duisberg was a man of action and didn't stop at lobbying alone. He gave a fillip to the development of different poisonous gases and would go to the labs himself to test their effectiveness. He was so involved with the cause that he later produced poisonous gases and protective gear under his own company Bayer's brand name.

This industriousness got further strengthened by the association of Fritz Haber, the Nobel Prize–winning chemist. He is considered the father of chemical warfare and was the head of the Kaiser Wilhelm Institute at that time. The Duisberg–Haber duo was very committed and took up the task of developing chemical weapons that could be used in war. Within a year, in January 1915, Haber was able to zero in on the gas to be used for his new chemical weapon: chlorine. It was Haber who came up with the idea that this gas was not to be exploded like a bomb, but discharged from cylinders. It was on his advice that a staggering 500 tons of chlorine was released from 2,000 cylinders on the Allied forces from 22–24 April. Despite this, Haber was enraged, as he felt that the German armed forces had not taken him seriously.

His grudge was that the German officers did not provide the necessary thrust that was needed to make inroads into the Allied formations on the back of the chlorine attack. He registered his protest, writing, 'You cannot win a war only with chemical weapons. You need a good ground army support as well.'

_____

the factory's war work: gas being made, shales being filled, gas masks being assembled … etc.'

Haber was frustrated at not getting the expected results from the chemical attack on the western front and returned home to Berlin a disappointed man. Meanwhile, his reputation had spread far and wide, and people realized the inhuman nature of Germany's war effort. Among them was Haber's wife, Clara. She was shaken by her husband's cruel act and pleaded with him to quit his work, trying every means to dissuade him. But he was steadfast and said, 'We have to kill the enemy at any cost and the means are not important. We can use any method to annihilate the enemy on a large scale and as quickly as possible.' Her fervent appeals fell on deaf ears, and he left for the warfront within the next fifteen days.

This time, it was the eastern front against Russia, which was attacked by Germany with chemical weapons 64 km from Warsaw. Russia was worse off compared to the Allied forces, and the soldiers had no means to protect themselves from chemical attacks. Moreover, even nature was working against them with the strong winds posing another challenge. Haber was happy because this meant that the chlorine cloud would spread wider and cause more harm. Everything worked out the way he wished, and almost the entire Siberian regiment was wiped out in the first attack itself. There were thirty-nine officers and 4,310 soldiers in the regiment, and after the attack, only four officers and forty soldiers remained. It was now crystal clear to most people, including Clara Haber, that these chemical weapons could not be stopped. She realized that the game her husband had started would only get more severe, monstrous and heinous with time. But she could still stop herself from being a mute witness. While Haber was busy celebrating killing off thousands of enemy soldiers with his chemical attacks, Clara shot herself dead in her home in Berlin the same night.

Hitler used Haber's research to build his torture camps. The Nazis were able to estimate the number of people they could kill in one go using these poisonous gases. But as they say, 'Those who live by the sword die by the sword.' That is exactly what happened with Haber. In 1934, he was banished by Hitler because he was a Jew. Haber couldn't digest the humiliation. He had been conferred a national honour in Germany for his services during the First World War, but had become unwanted in his own country just years later. This was unbearable for Haber and he left Germany a bitter man. He took off to Switzerland and fell sick with some unidentified disease and died there as an unknown, faceless man.

Chemical warfare had claimed another victim in such a bizarre manner!

While so much was happening, Britain couldn't just sit and watch. Efforts were being made on a war-footing to come up with something effective as retaliation. On 26 May 1915, Army Chief John French called for Major Charles Howard Foulkes and appointed him the chief advisor for gas warfare.[9] It was not like he knew a lot about gases, but he was versatile and hard-working. He was born in India and had spent twenty-three years in the British army, having served in Sierra Leone, Gambia, Gold Coast, West Indies, South Africa and other places. Most of these nations were in the grip of some disease or other. He had survived two bouts of malaria in Sierra Leone. He was a part of the First Boer War and had narrowly escaped being killed on at least half a dozen occasions. Since he had managed to survive in such tough places, the British army generals must have thought that he would be capable of showing the way towards a new chemical gas. Once he was appointed, his mission was clear: to develop an effective gas weapon, and fast. The media had begun training its guns on the government, and the *London Times* had started printing graphic photos of soldiers who had died due to chemical gas attacks. They wrote in detail about how bodies would turn blue-black, how they frothed at the mouth and so on. Readers

---

9   Ibid., pp. 9–11.

felt uneasy and sick reading the gory descriptions. The *Daily Mail* went a step further and asked British women to make masks of cloth or cotton. The very next day, the *Mail* office was inundated with 10 lakh masks, and the government was burdened with the task of sending them to the warfront. Nobody was sure if they would be effective, but they had to respect public sentiments. Soon enough, they realized that not only were these masks ineffective, they were a hindrance because the gas would get absorbed by the material and make breathing difficult.

Someone suggested that the soldiers should soak the masks in soda and wear them, but that too made no difference. On the contrary, their masks would go dry and they would get tired soaking them repeatedly. It was clear that chlorine gas could penetrate these masks. The soldiers continued to die. Finally, the government decided to ban these masks and buried them for good along with the dead bodies of the soldiers.

Foulkes's next strategy was more frightening than the masks. He assembled a team of young British chemists and paid them attractive salaries. The team accumulated 5,500 cylinders of chlorine, weighing a total of 150 tons, by 25 September 1915, to be used against the Germans in Loos, Belgium. The cylinders were ferried to the battlefield by boats patrolled by planes, carried discreetly in unmarked containers labelled 'the accessory' with utmost secrecy. Anyone who accidentally used the word 'gas' instead was severely penalized.

Despite all the planning and care, the British were outwitted by nature. The usual 5 a.m. morning breeze that blew towards the German camp suddenly turned direction and began blowing towards the British front. Some of the young British soldiers got scared and refused to open the cylinders. One of Foulkes's commanders lit a cigarette and insisted that the smoke was indeed drifting in the direction of the Germans, but very few of his soldiers fell for his deception. Some did agree to open the cylinder valves, but they did not have spanners of the right size. After scrambling around borrowing spanners, finally only two cylinders could be opened. As expected, the gas fumes from the cylinders drifted back towards the British soldiers, laying hordes of them flat. Eventually, the wind changed direction and the gas did drift towards the Germans, but they had already been warned. They opened fire on the British with their machine guns, damaging a lot of the gas cylinders, filling the British trenches and causing havoc. Foulkes described the episode in his diary saying, 'If fortune had been a little kinder, and the wind had been only slightly more favorable, we would have gained a smashing victory on this day.'

Alas, that was not to be. The Allies were soon to face another challenge: a chemical attack that was the brainchild of the treacherous German Dr Anton Dilger, who worked secretly for Germany while he was living in the US. His father, Hubert Dilger, was not only a noted American citizen but also a decorated military officer who had received the Medal of Honor for his work as an artilleryman at the Battle of Chancellorsville (1863) during the US Civil War. Hence, no one suspected that his son would work against the US.

Anton was born in Virginia, where his parents lived after moving out of Ohio soon after the American Civil War. Anton left for Germany when he was nine years old, and studied in Heidelberg, Munich, Bensheim and several other places. He later joined Heidelberg University and began to teach while he was studying surgery. His work involved growing animal cells using tissue culture. He wasn't very successful initially, but he did get his PhD degree in 1912. This was the time of the Balkan war (1912–13)—there is no clear idea about the role he played in that war. Some historians believed that he worked as a surgeon in the Bulgarian Medical Corps, while others believed that he worked with the German Red Cross.

But these claims and counterclaims had no bearing on his upcoming achievements.

Nevertheless, it was a fact that Anton was in Germany at the start of the First World War and returned to the US within a year, armed with deadly cultures of diseases like anthrax and glanders. Glanders, also known as equina, farcy and droes, is a disease that predominantly affects horses, mules and donkeys. If left uncontrolled, it can affect cats, dogs and goats. The typical symptoms of glanders include the formation of nodular lesions in the lungs and ulceration of the mucous membranes in the upper respiratory tract. With time, there is a dry cough, fever and the release of an infectious nasal discharge, followed by septicemia and death within days. Death can occur within months, and survivors act as carriers. Glanders epidemics are common in the poor nations of Africa, West Asia, and Central and South America. Later, this disease spread to humans as well, due to contact with infected animals. It was proved that it was caused by a bacterium called Burkholder mallei.[10] Since it originated in an animal, it was classified as a zoonotic agent.

Once it was certain that glanders could affect both animals and humans, many scientists felt that it had the potential to be used in biological warfare as horses, mules and donkeys were used for transportation of arms, ammunition and other supplies during wartime. Anton played a pioneering role in this regard. He was so keen on doing something worthwhile for his country that he was ready to go to any length and was least concerned with the harm it could cause. No doubts were raised given his US passport and his father's reputation. Hence, he could set foot in the US armed with cultures of *Bacillus Anthracis* and *Burkholder Mallei*. He set up a laboratory in the basement of his brother Carl's house in the

10   William James, *Andrews' Diseases of the Skin: Clinical Dermatology.*

north of Washington. It was no less than a slaughterhouse where he experimented on novel ways to kill animals. [11]

What Anton and his associates went on to do showed their immorality and cruelty. He and his brother used horses and donkeys from around their area as guinea pigs. They would smear the noses of the animals with a mixture containing the disease-causing bacteria, and soon enough, the animals fell sick. Once the brothers were certain that their plan was working, they got the stable owners of the area to work for them, giving them bottles filled with the germs saying that they were vaccines for the animals. The innocent stablehands followed the instructions sincerely, and several healthy animals died.

Anton returned to Germany in the second half of 1916 after his experiments with animals were successful. He returned to the US the very next year. Meanwhile, the Federal Bureau of Investigation (FBI), the country's premier investigating agency, had grown suspicious. FBI agents began tailing him, and once he realized that he was under scrutiny, Anton fled to neighbouring Mexico and began living there under a false name. When he felt that his cover could be blown, he moved further away to Madrid in Spain, taking on the name Alberto Dondo. He kept in constant touch with his motherland, Germany.

But changing names cannot change destiny, and Anton would have to face the consequences. He was afflicted by a lethal disease similar to the ones he himself had worked on spreading. Whatever the source may have been, Anton fell prey to the Spanish flu and died on 17 October 1918 at the age of thirty-four, far away from his motherland. He must have attracted the curse of the thousands of animals that died of mysterious illnesses in Romania, Norway, Spain

---

11   See Robert Koenig, *The Fourth Horseman* for details about Dilger's role in the First World War.

and other countries. Though he didn't play a direct role there, his method of spreading disease had caught on, and many people were using the same means to cause widespread havoc. Newer ideas were devised, like smearing gloves used for handling animals with germs, or mixing germs with animal feed. The purpose of all these efforts was the same: to kill enemy soldiers and their animals. The innocent animals had to die only because they were born in warring countries! There is no record of the number of animals that died as a result of the inhuman practices during the First World War.

When discussions about the weapons that needed to be barred were taking place after the First World War, no country felt the need to ban chemicals and biological weapons used to kill animals. It was as if animals were meant to either be killed on the battlefield or be used as guinea pigs in labs!

The animal deaths may not have been a big deal then, but the world was forced to take note of the wounds of a single man who swore never to use such lethal chemicals ever again. They had almost rendered him blind for a short time. He was shaken, but the sentiment was short-lived. The moment he got his eyesight back, he forgot how he had been affected and resumed the annihilation of mankind with renewed energy and fervour.

His name was Adolf Hitler, the Führer of Germany.

3

The Reign of Chemical Gases

GERMANY'S enemy nations began competing with one another to see which of them could inflict the maximum harm on it. They began planning different ways of defeating Germany and exploring ways to produce chemical gases and biological weapons as quickly as possible. These countries were initially opposed to using chemical weapons and were all aware that they couldn't progress further without disregarding the Hague accord. England had actually tried to pay the Germans back in the same coin in the battle at Loos,[12] but it had backfired despite it capturing 3,000 German soldiers and seizing a dozen German tanks. The losses were greater than the gains. Almost 50,000 British soldiers lost their lives in the Loos battle and around 2,000 were killed by their own chemical gas weapons.

---

12 Robert Harris and Jeremy Paxman, *A Higher Form of Killing*, pp. 14–15.

England wanted to avenge this irreparable loss by causing severe damage to Germany. It needed something to match the German chlorine attack; for the time being, producing more chlorine seemed to be the only answer, and that is what the Allied countries decided to focus on. But they erred in thinking that the extent of the German violence would stop with chlorine.

To halt the German march, preparation was needed at two levels. The first was devising a way to survive a gas attack and the second was developing an equally deadly weapon. The Allies began working on both on a war footing, and chemical research labs were set up in England and France where anyone with knowledge of chemistry was employed. Experiments were on in full swing, and the effort to find a chemical weapon and teach Germany a lesson was so intense that even mere descriptions of their methods are spine-chilling even to this day.

The British ministry of war set up a 3,000 acre laboratory for chemical production and testing at Salisbury.[13] It was expanded further over a year and became almost as big as a village. There were shabby little houses with residents who knew exactly what they were doing and what they were being used for. Nevertheless, they were ready to take the risk. Since such things were unheard of those days, the residents and employees of the facility had innumerable questions like: What did testing involve? What did it mean to test harmful chemicals on oneself? What if they died in the process? But the head of the physiology department, Joseph Barcroft, was least concerned.[14] He had completely engrossed himself in the development of chemical weapons. Barcroft had heard that the French laboratory had tested hydrogen cyanide, with inconclusive

---

13   Jeanne Guillemin, *Biological Weapons: From the Invention of State-Sponsored Programs to Contemporary Bioterrorism*, pp. 40–44.

14   Robert Harris and Jeremy Paxman, *A Higher Form of Killing*, pp. 39–41.

results. They had not figured out the concentration of the gas that would be required to kill a human being. After testing the gas on dogs, they found that the dogs did die, but not all at the same time. Barcroft decided to test the gas on himself. He shut himself along with his dog in a room filled with hydrogen cyanide, armed with a stopwatch. The moment he entered the room, he was hit by the gas, but he focused his attention on the dog. Within 30 seconds, it struggled to walk even two steps. Barcroft moved about the room, and the dog, cursed by loyalty, followed suit. In 55 seconds, the dog collapsed to the ground and began showing signs of respiratory distress typical of cyanide poisoning. Another 20 seconds later, it stopped breathing and was dead. Barcroft brought the dog out of the room and conducted his autopsy. The conclusion was that a concentration of 1:2000 hydrogen cyanide was enough to kill a dog weighing 30 kg in 1 minute and 35 seconds. Hence, the concentration had to be almost doubled to kill a person double that weight.

Barcroft was hesitant to jump to such conclusions. He only felt giddy and nauseous once he came out of the room, nothing more. His simple, straightforward observation was that the concentration of the gas had to be much stronger in order to kill a human. His bravery was appreciated by none other than King George V himself, and he prayed for Barcroft's health and long life. Not just the king, even Prime Minister Lloyd George wrote to Barcroft expressing his admiration for his gallantry and service to mankind.

An unexpected incident happened when one of Barcroft's assistants was travelling by train with a canister of poison gas. All of a sudden, the canister began to leak. She wondered how she could stop the train or what she would say that wouldn't hurt this clandestine operation. She took her scarf, tied the canister to it and hung it outside a window of the running train. The canister had emptied by the time she reached her destination. Nothing much happened, except that the passengers in the coach behind her suffered unexplained bouts of vomiting. Fortunately, the poison gas did not prove fatal and the passengers never got to know the real reason for their sickness. If not, the consequences could have been unimaginably serious!

Not everyone survived such dangerous experiments. Colonel Watson, head of the Allies' Central Laboratory in France, died as a result of tests he conducted on himself. He was investigating the time taken for the poison gases to take effect once they were inhaled. Colonel Harrison, the deputy controller of the British Chemical Warfare Committee, too died a similar death.

These are the names that have been recorded. The real number of deaths due to human experimentation must have been in the thousands. These testing methods were extremely dangerous and primitive, and it wasn't possible to move forward without them. If these efforts weren't made, Germany would have been left behind. It was important for the nation to find a chemical weapon at any cost, and a large number of people were involved in the search for it. Human guinea pigs were made to sit in circular trenches as cylinders of poisonous gases were released. Observers wearing prototype masks would stand behind them and note down how long the guinea pigs could withstand the gas. They observed symptoms like the irritation in the eyes, the change in colour of the skin, and others. Skin exposed to the gas would get singed, sometimes peeling off like cucumber skin on first exposure. All these details were unknown till then, and naturally there were no antidotes for treatment!

People suffered severely, and with time, both the general public and the military establishment were agitated and began expressing their outrage openly. As a result, there were hardly any human volunteers available for these experiments, and laboratories began employing drivers, cooks and watchmen for testing. What unimaginable things people had to do to make a living!

When even they became unavailable, scientists turned their attention towards animals. Cats, dogs, rats, goats, guinea pigs, monkeys, rabbits and frogs were used for poison gas tests. All these animals had one thing in common: there was no one to raise their voice on their behalf. Human volunteers were only exposed to the poison gases in enclosed spaces, but when it came to animals, gases were squirted on to their faces, chemicals were injected into them, and they were placed in chambers filled with gas. Even their food was mixed with poisonous chemicals. The sole purpose of these experiments was to find out how long the animals took to die!

Simultaneously, newer types of masks were being designed for human use.[15] Their outer layers were made of different kinds of materials to test their effectiveness against poisonous gases. Soldiers were trained to wear the masks within six seconds of the gas alarms being sounded. Some of the masks were very heavy, cumbersome and uncomfortable. A few had elephant-like trunks hanging down from the mouth. These were connected to oxygen cylinders tied to the soldiers' backs. Some masks had chemicals applied inside them. One of them was sodium hyposulphate and these helmets were called 'hypo helmets'.

The other kind of helmet was the 'P helmet', so called because it had sodium phenolate inside it. These chemicals would mix with sweat in summers and trickle down, stinging the wearer's face and neck. The first few prototypes of these masks produced a feeling of suffocation because there was no vent for the exhaled air to escape, causing dangerous concentrations of carbon dioxide to build up inside. The eyepieces would get steamed up and make even walking difficult!

Some soldiers were so vexed that death seemed a better choice than this torture, but they had no idea that even death wouldn't be the end. There was a big demand for soldiers' corpses and organs, which were brought to the laboratory at Porton, where a section of

---

15   Ibid., pp. 18–20.

the Royal Medical Corps would study the cadavers to ascertain the real time and cause of death and record its findings. Simultaneously, the war was also on, with a new front being opened in France. The Germans continued their novel ways of killing people and a selected few of these corpses were brought to Porton. The Allies were hopeful of finding something worthwhile, but they faced a severe blow: a new, fatal poison gas!

At 5.30 a.m. on 19 December, the German Gas Corps surprised the British front with an attack at Ypres, using a new gas. Not chlorine; chorine was visible and hence offered a chance to escape. But the Germans had been looking for some poison gas that could not be detected, and they found their answer in phosgene. When the attack happened, Captain Adie of the Royal Army Medical Corps was having tea. He heard a loud hissing sound and realized something was wrong. He immediately sounded the gas alarms and an emergency was declared, but it was of no use. Phosgene travelled at a very high speed and reached the Allied division 8 km away. The men in the trenches at the front lines had no chance of survival. Captain Adie tried his best to save the lives of several soldiers, but some died on the way and others in hospitals. At least forty men lost their lives in front of his eyes. The impact of phosgene was so strong that it soon filled the entire Allied territory.

Phosgene was eighteen times more powerful than chlorine, so much so that even 1:50,000 concentrations caused lethal delayed effects. Unlike chlorine, phosgene caused no immediate harm. Victims who had inhaled lethal doses felt nothing other than a mild soreness in the throat and irritation in the eyes. They didn't even realize they had ingested a poisonous substance. On the contrary, they actually felt euphoric soon after inhaling the gas and worked with enthusiasm and energy for about two days. After that, their lungs filled up with fluid, and once they were completely choked, even a slight action like turning over in bed proved disastrous.

Blood pressure shot up and the heart rate increased up to 120 beats per minute. Soon, there would be a total collapse.

Captain Adie and his associates tried to help several victims. It was recorded that all of them were vomiting repeatedly and every hour almost four glasses of fluid were being expelled from their lungs. This was called the 'drowning period', after which the victims died within forty-eight hours. 1,069 men had been attacked by the gas that day and 116 of them died within the next two to three days.

It took the Allied forces one year to equip themselves to fight such an attack. They too produced phosgene and used it to attack the Germans in the battle of Somme in June 1916. They mixed chlorine with phosgene and released the toxic gas mixture over a 17-mile-long battle line. It created an enormous cloud over a large area and everything living that came under its effect, perished—horses, humans, insects, wildlife and even trees!

The war correspondent of the daily *Frankfurter* reached Somme in three days' time and reported: 'The affected area is covered with the corpses of soldiers and the carcasses of animals. Even rats and mice lay dead in the trenches after gas attacks. Dead grasshoppers, wild insects, butterflies are strewn all over the area. Only two species seem to be unaffected by the poisonous gas: sparrows and owls. They will not have to struggle for food anymore.'

Contrastingly, the *Daily Chronicle* of England enthusiastically reported: 'Every single German in that area had been killed by our gas attack.' In the first eighteen days of the Somme battle, the Allies carried out a staggering fifty gas attacks and used almost 1,560 tons of phosgene in all. It became the main chemical weapon in the years to come.

The effects that were once seen with chlorine were now happening with phosgene. The only difference was that until then, the Germans, who were using it to kill, were now becoming the victims! The harmful effects of phosgene lingered on, such as loss of appetite, persistent nausea and a general sense of dejection. Its delayed reactions caused many casualties among the men of the Special Companies. Although the soldiers were not too scared of phosgene, fear had begun to grip the common man.

Intentionally or otherwise, what was happening was inevitable. The military generals had decided that this was the path they had to take. On one side was the war foisted on them and on the other, the annoyance of the people at large. The British military establishment was caught between the two and they decided to have a public relations programme to allay any apprehensions citizens had about Britain's war strategy. The chemical weapons laboratories and the military headquarters were opened to the public once a week, and the military chiefs were ordered to be present. They organized lectures and interactions with reputed personalities and scientists at these venues. George Bernard Shaw was one of the prominent visitors, while the Duke of Westminster and members of the royal family were more than ready to be a part of the initiative. Among the most important personalities who spent an entire day at Helfaut, a commune in France, and tried to understand what was happening was Winston Churchill. According to reports, Churchill was mighty impressed with the progress in chemical warfare and expressed his appreciation for the efforts being made. He was to play a major role in this regard in the future. The public relations exercise proved to be successful, and almost every chemist in Britain became involved in the gas warfare efforts some way or the other.[16]

Over a thousand senior scientists and soldiers worked day and night at the central laboratory at Porton Down. In the following months, thirty-three designated British laboratories tested 1,50,000 organic and inorganic compounds in an attempt to develop the most poisonous war gas possible. The results of this massive search

---

16 Ibid., pp. 23–25; Jeanne Guillemin, *Biological Weapons*, pp. 44–53.

began showing on the battlefields. In 1915, 3,600 tons of gas were discharged, and that figure more than quadrupled to 15,000 tons in 1916. Poisonous gases were gaining importance rapidly, and were competing with airplanes developed only sixteen years ago. Defence experts were divided on what was more effective: chemical warfare or airplanes.

There were two events in Britain that substantiated the efficacy of chemical warfare. Till then, poisonous gases were released using cylinders, and chemical weapons were not shot at enemies. The gases had to be supported by wind to be effective, or else they would go waste or prove counterproductive, like it happened in Loos. Hence, they weren't always reliable. It was important to minimize the effect of nature from the gas attack equation.

This was made possible by the Livens projector, invented by Captain F.H. Livens, a civil engineer[17] who had joined the army, driven by his pathological hatred for the Germans. He was bent on finding ways to crush them. Livens was the commander of the British special brigade and was ready to use any means to kill the enemy. He created a simple but extremely effective device to fire chemical gases at the enemy.

The projector consisted of a steel tube, three to four feet long and 8 inches in diameter. It was simply buried in the ground at an angle of 45 degrees and fired remotely using electrical charge produced from the attached batteries. The charge sent hurtling from the tube a drum containing 30 pounds of chemical gases, usually pure phosgene. Instead of releasing the cloud of gas from cylinders, which placed them at the mercy of the wind, the Livens projector made it possible to virtually drop gas cylinders on the heads of the enemy. The projector was not very accurate, but it had the range of

---

17   Robert Harris and Jeremy Paxman, *A Higher Form of Killing*, pp. 24, 25, 44–49.

1 mile, and was also inexpensive and easy to make. Twenty-five such gas bombs could be released at a time. The Livens projector was cumbersome to use because the twenty-five bombs had to be fixed to those pipes and buried into the ground at the correct angle, and then the batteries had to be connected to each of them. But this was an agony that had to be endured in order to kill enemies and also keep oneself safe. According to Livens's calculation, 'If the projector was mass-manufactured, the cost of killing Germans would be reduced to only sixteen shillings apiece.'

The British first launched a full-scale attack using the Livens projector at the battle of Arras on 9 April 1917. The day's report went: 'The discharge took place practically simultaneously: a dull red flash seemed to flicker all along the front as far as the eye could reach, and there was a slight ground tremor, followed a little later by a muffled roar, as 1,340 of these sinister projectiles hurtled through space, turning clumsily over and over, and some of them, no doubt, colliding with each other in flight. About twenty seconds later, they landed in masses into the German positions, and after a brief pause the steel cases burst open by the explosive charges inside, and nearly fifty tons of liquid phosgene were released which vaporized instantly and formed a cloud so dense that Livens, who watched the discharge from an airplane, noticed that the cloud was so thick that the villages below became invisible.'

The attack had produced the desired results. This was the first time since the First World War that the Allies had hit the Germans so badly. Germany's arrogance was crushed and they had to think of defence strategies for the first time. The Allies were obviously enthused by their victory and the British created a newer version of the Livens projector in which steel pipes were used at a specific angle and small projectiles were created. These could be used to launch small bombs 4 inches in diameter. When thousands of them were used simultaneously, it appeared to be raining bombs.

These were not the usual bombs but gas bombs with 2 litres of gas in each.

The extent of damage caused by these was beyond imagination. England began changing the chemicals and gases used in these bombs with the explicit intention not to kill the enemy but to maim or threaten them. Depending on the purpose, they used bone oil or amyl acetate. Both smelt obnoxious and the stink stayed for a long time. The Germans would panic thinking that anything they were attacked with was a lethal substance. The use of cylinders had become passé and by 1918, 94 per cent of the gas used was delivered using such bombs. According to one report, 6 crore and 60 lakh gas bombs had been used. All rules and regulations had been disregarded and these bombs delivered exceptional results for the Allies. The Germans were all at sea and had no clue about how they could retaliate. But soon, they were to come out all guns blazing with a deadly, inhuman chemical weapon.

The battleground of choice was again Ypres. At around 10 p.m. on the evening of 12 July 1917, the 15th and 55th British divisions came under heavy bombardment from the Germans.[18] The enemy was attacking with 77 mm and 105 mm gas shells. These weren't the gas shells that the soldiers were used to, and what was released was a sticky, brown liquid which gave off a smell variously described as 'unpleasant', 'oily', 'like garlic' and 'like mustard'. Apart from a slight irritation in the eyes and throat, there were no initial effects. Most of the soldiers quickly went back to sleep, but the peace lasted only for five to six hours. In the wee hours of the morning, they began to wake up with 'intolerable pain' in the eyes, which felt as though sand or grit had been rubbed into them. Then they began to vomit uncontrollably and lost their voice because their voice box was damaged. As the night wore on, the pain in the eyes became so

18   Ibid., pp. 26–30.

intense that many had to be given morphia, the predecessor of the modern-day morphine. Every organ and body part that had come in contact with the substance swelled up and formed extremely painful blisters on the backs of the thighs, buttocks and even the scrotum. As hours passed, the symptoms worsened, and moist, red patches of skin affected by the vapour turned into massive yellow blisters the colour of mustard flowers.

This was mustard gas or dichlorethyl sulphide, the deadliest and most toxic gas used till date! The liquid would stick to the ground and was almost invisible. Anyone who came in contact with it would feel irritation. It would freeze in cold weather and stay in the soil. The effects of mustard gas bombs used in 1917 stayed for almost a year, which meant that the entire affected area had to be sealed off. It was absorbed even through the skin and the effects worsened in case the skin was moist or sensitive. Another speciality of mustard gas was that it proved toxic even from long distances and caused the same symptoms and deaths. One instance is sufficient to describe its toxicity.

The autopsy of a British soldier exposed to mustard gas took ten days, and the remnants of the gas in dead bodies stung doctors even then. The chemical weapons advisory division of the British army collected shards of these bombs for examination and they too experienced irritation throughout their bodies. One fact was clear from the autopsies—those who inhaled the mustard gas lost their voice boxes and had their wind pipes damaged. The only sounds that escaped their throats were moans and groans. Their lungs filled with blood and their hearts swelled.

Victims who thought they had survived the attack would discover severe secondary infections of the respiratory system and the skin after two or three weeks had passed. The list of symptoms was staggering! Huge blisters on the hands, scalp, shoulders, arms, abdomen, buttocks, genitals, thighs, legs and feet;

erythema, iritis, scrotal dermatitis, leucodermia, conjunctivitis, pharyngitis, bronchitis, tracheitis, gastritis, pleurodynia, purulent bronchopneumonia, acute rhinitis (bleeding from the nose); debility, gastric pain, mental inertia, chronic cough, breathlessness, memory weakness and defective eyesight—the list was endless! The victims would be extremely stressed owing to the severity of the symptoms and their lives would become torturous. Those who survived would panic seeing the suffering of their peers and lose their will to live.

Just two days after the attack, field hospitals were choked with casualties, echoing with the heart-wrenching moans and groans of the patients. There was no limit to the agony and pain the victims had to endure. The symptoms were so severe and the pain so unbearable that several affected soldiers contemplated suicide. The pain in the eyes was most intolerable. Eyes wouldn't open and victims would go temporarily blind. There was no cure, and the only thing they could do was tie a wet cloth over their eyes. Many had to be given morphine injections to alleviate the pain, but even that provided only short-term relief. A few days later, the blisters on the body would burst, get infected and refuse to heal. There was no end to the intense misery, and even death wouldn't come fast. The victims suffered for ten days before death could relieve them of the pain. The suffering was so extreme that they had to be tied to their beds to keep them from attempting suicide.

The doctors and nurses too underwent a lot of trauma. Vera Brittain, a nurse who was assigned to a ward with mustard gas victims, noted in her diary: 'I wish those people who talk about going on with this war at any cost could see the soldiers suffering from mustard gas poisoning. Huge mustard-coloured blisters, blind eyes, all sticky and stuck together, always fighting for breath, with voices a mere whisper, saying that their throats are closing and they know they will choke … It will help stop the war soon.'

But nothing like that happened—chemical weapons had become a mainstay of war. Germany produced massive quantities of mustard gas and used it extensively. It delayed attacks until enormous reserves of mustard gas had been built up.

Within ten days, the Allied positions were pounded with more than a million shells containing 2,500 tons of gas. By the end of the first week, the number of gassed men admitted to British medical units was 2,934; by the end of the second week, a further 6,476 had been added; by the end of the third week, another 4,886. In all, from July 1917 to the end of the war, British casualties from mustard gas amounted to at least 1,25,000—70 per cent of the total number of British gas casualties for the entire war. One in six deaths during the past year and a half of the First World War was due to mustard gas.

Although the Germans were at the forefront of the gas attacks, the Allies had the last laugh. France began producing mustard gas at a very large scale, with scores of French chemical companies, chemists and scientists involved in the effort. Britain too was trying to get into mustard gas production, but to their misfortune, although British chemists had suggested that dichloroethyl sulphide be used as a chemical weapon months before the Germans thought about it, the British government had rejected their proposal. According to them, it wasn't as lethal as they desired.

However, the government woke up after Germany killed thousands of British soldiers and swung into action. Bulk production of the gas was an arduous, complicated and dangerous process, and the British lost precious time in setting up factories. Among its 1,400 workers, there had been over 110 illnesses directly attributable to gas production. In addition, there were 160 accidents, and three people were killed and another four died of related illnesses in the first six months. Despite the frenzied efforts, British mustard gas supplies reached the battlefield only in September 1918, just two months before the end of the war.

But the British couldn't wait any more. The war was at their doorstep and they decided to use any means possible. Cylinders of phosgene were mounted on the backs of railway engines, and trucks were loaded with tankers of phosgene with the lids left open. As a result, almost 19 km of land that came in the way of these trucks and railway engines were devastated. Animals, birds and humans were killed; trees and grass were bleached. In March 1918, the Allies attacked the Germans with 2 lakh cylinders, totalling 6,000 tons of phosgene from a dozen railway trains. There was chlorine too. But despite all their efforts, they didn't get the expected results.

The German spirit was still high and they surprised the Allies by signing a peace pact with Russia. A much-strengthened German army was now able to launch its own offensive in the west. The large chemical conglomerate IG increased its production several times over and the Germans blanketed the British on four successive nights, from 10–14 March, with 1,50,000 bombs of mustard gas—7,000 British soldiers fell victim. Simultaneously, the Germans boosted their ranks and attacked deep into the British camp.

In advancing so far, however, Germany had sown the seeds of its own defeat. In July and August, the Allies were able to strike back at the overextended German positions. Their armies too were heavily dependent on chemicals. The Allies became stronger with the arrival of the US troops. The French were ready with their supply of mustard gas, and the British too had their stocks at hand.

The Allies began their incessant mustard gas attack, and on 14 October, during the final Allied offensive, British mustard shells rained down into a Belgian village called Werwick, causing heavy casualties among the 16th Bavarian Reserve Infantry. All those who survived were seriously wounded. They were loaded into trains and shipped back to Germany. Among them, blinded and humiliated, was a twenty-nine-year-old corporal who could see the defeat of the Germans clearly despite being blindfolded. He swore to avenge the German defeat and teach the British a lesson. Almost two decades later, the young man got his chance. That wounded, nearly blind soldier went on to become the German dictator Adolf Hitler.[19]

---

19   Ibid., pp. 32–34.

4

The Poison Trap

THE First World War had come to an end, and its casualties far outnumbered that of other wars, thanks to the use of chemical weapons, about 1,13,000 tons in all. According to official records, close to 13,00,000 people had been affected, of which 91,000 lost their lives. But these records are not complete. The details of the dead and wounded in the April 1915 battle at Ypres are not available. Furthermore, records of other gas attacks which are politically inconvenient do not exist. Many countries destroyed all evidence of their use of chemical weapons. Obviously, there were far more victims of chemical warfare than those recorded. Many soldiers who fell victim to gas attacks were only recorded as casualties of war, and their real cause of death was never documented.

In fact, the post-war sentiment should have been that the perpetrators of this inhumanity should be brought to book, but nothing like that ever happened. On the contrary, the person responsible for the development of these chemical weapons, Fritz Haber, was awarded the Nobel Prize for Chemistry in 1919 for his work on the synthesis of ammonia. Fearing that he would be tried as a war criminal, Fritz Haber grew a beard and went away to Switzerland under a false name after the war. He had never imagined that he would win the Nobel Prize. In fact, the Nobel committee came under severe criticism for their decision[20] and the *New York Times* wrote: 'Why only the Chemistry Prize ... Why was the Nobel Prize for literature too not given to the man who wrote a new chapter in human cruelty and inhumanity?'

But the outrage ended there. In reality, almost all countries were following the path shown by Haber and setting up laboratories for manufacturing poisonous gases. The entire world was falling into the trap.

The US went a few steps ahead of Haber, conducting a lot of experiments. A team based at Catholic University, Washington, DC, discovered Lewisite. It was faster-acting than mustard gas and caused an 'immediate, excruciating pain' upon striking. The victims would experience severe pricking pain in the eyes and the skin would peel off like boiled potatoes. The first batch of 150 tons of Lewisite was at sea, on its way to Europe, and had the war not ended, it would have been used by the Allies.

Meanwhile, the world's largest poison gas manufacturing facility came up in the US near Ohio. This was probably the largest research organization ever assembled for one specific objective—1,200 technical men and 700 service assistants researching into more than 4,000 potentially poisonous substances. The entire complex consisted of 218 manufacturing buildings, 30 km of railway, 20 km of roadway and 18 km of high-tension electrical transmission lines. The entire project had cost around $45 million dollars. If needed, its factories were capable of producing 2,00,000 chemical bombs and shells per day.

---

20   Robert Harris and Jeremy Paxman, *A Higher Form of Killing*, pp. 34–36.

In Europe, Italy established a *servizio chemico militare*, an independent manufacturing facility, around the same time. The main French chemical warfare installation was the Atelier de Pyrotechnie du Bouchet near Paris. In Asia, the Japanese navy began work on chemical weapons, while the Germans, despite losing the war, increased the scale of poison gas manufacturing. Germany built its own device, 'Gaswerfer 1918', for gas attacks, on the lines of the British Livens projector. These could be used to launch a barrage of phosgene bombs.

England too developed an 'M device', which used the extremely poisonous arsenic smoke to penetrate the most effective masks within 15 seconds. The victim suffered severe agony within a minute. Once the gas reached the lungs, it caused extreme pain in the head, coupled with mental distress. Some soldiers poisoned by these substances temporarily went raving mad, and tried to burrow into the ground to escape from imaginary pursuers. It was a tough challenge managing the victims.

Details of the extent to which these poisonous chemicals affected the human body and mind started coming out slowly but surely. People were able to gauge the economic losses that ensued. England almost went bankrupt arranging for disability pensions for the soldiers affected by the gas attacks. In the first year itself, it had to pay pensions and compensations for almost 19,000 soldiers. The figure only increased with time. It had to continue paying victims till 1970. The actual number of victims was kept secret. The British government kept a firm control over these matters, and there was a strict ban on gas attack victims writing their memoirs and autobiographies. Despite the economic fallout, the manufacture of chemical weapons continued unabated. The regulation was only on the disclosure of details!

The Treaty of Versailles came into force after the First World War, in 1919, and the Allied powers described chemical weapons as a 'prohibited' form of warfare and banned the import and manufacture of poison gas in Germany. There was a lot of discussion on what had to be done with these weapons. Three years later, the Washington Treaty went even further and the 'civilized powers' decreed that banning of chemical warfare should 'be universally accepted as part of international law binding alike to the conscience and practice of nations'.

In May 1925, under the auspices of the League of Nations (an earlier avatar of the United Nations), a conference on the international arms trade was convened in Geneva. Led by the US, the delegates unanimously agreed to try and tackle the problem of poison gas with the hope of reducing the barbarity of modern warfare. After a month of wrangling in legal and military committees—during which the Polish delegation prophetically suggested that they also ban the use of germ weapons, which had not been developed till then—the delegates came together on 17 June to sign, what remains to this day, the strongest legal constraint on chemical and biological warfare. According to the treaty, the use in war of asphyxiating, poisonous or other gases, and of all analogous liquids, materials or devices, was prohibited. Thirty-eight countries including the US, France, Britain, Germany and Italy signed it.

The next step was implementing the treaty. The lobbies of chemical companies all over swung into action and began campaigning about how detrimental such a one-sided agreement could be. They garnered the support of veterans' associations and the American Chemical Society. They put forth the connection between the manufacture of chemical weapons and defence capabilities and convinced people at large that defence strategies would come to naught without chemical weapons. Several military organizations and unions of serving and retired military personnel came out in support of the continued manufacture of chemical weapons. Senators too joined the chorus, and soon enough the US had to withdraw from the Geneva Protocol. Japan followed suit and refused to ratify the treaty.

The European nations did not refuse en masse but adopted a more cautious approach. Many of the states which ratified the Geneva Protocol, including France, Great Britain and the USSR, did so only after adding two significant clauses. (1) The agreement would not be considered binding unless the country they were fighting had also ratified the protocol; (2) If any other country attacked them using chemical or biological weapons, they reserved the right to reply in kind.

Gradually, the terms of the treaty became very slack. Russia and Japan added further terms, and the Geneva Protocol remained, effectively, a ban only on the first use of poison gas or germs. But there was certainly no ban on researching and stockpiling of chemical weapons. Research included 'improvements' to many First World War weapons, including gas shells and mortar bombs. In short, the nations that signed the treaty ensured that it remained ineffective, and all of them continued to manufacture and amass chemical weapons for future use.

England set up a committee soon after the war to decide the future of the Porton Down chemical research and manufacturing facility and the policies regarding newer chemical weapons. The committee, which included General Foulkes, had to conduct a survey and present its findings. It concluded 'with no shadow of doubt' that gas is a legitimate weapon in war ... and that it will be used in the future may be taken as a foregone conclusion. It is imperative that Britain is prepared.'

That being the case, Britain decided to give its research efforts a fillip. Taking the risks and dangers associated with it into account, it offered hefty salaries, three months paid annual leave, and other allowances to those involved. The whole process was kept under wraps; testing and research on new chemical weapons went on at breakneck speed for twenty years from May 1919 till the start of the Second World War.

Along with testing and research, new chemicals were being tried on battlefields as well. One such testing ground was, unfortunately, India. In the latter half of 1919, General Foulkes was posted to India.[21] The first permission he sought from his government was for the use of chemical weapons against the Afghans and rebellious tribesmen on the North-West Frontier. The British government was hesitant but General Foulkes was in a hurry. He wrote to his government:

'Use of chemical weapons has become routine in warfare, and hence it wouldn't be immoral or unethical for us to do the same. What is more important is that these are not going to be used on the citizens of any particular nation but on nomadic tribesmen. The Hague treaty does not apply to these tribes.'

In short, it meant that people not bound by the borders of any country had no right to live like human beings.

General Foulkes's last argument hit home and proved decisive. The government granted him permission. Soon, stocks of phosgene and mustard gas were sent out, while British troops trained in anti-gas suits in the scorching heat of the Khyber Pass during summer. Large supplies of smoke shells were stored at Peshawar near the Afghan frontier to flush out rebellious tribesmen from their mountain hideouts. The British had such a nonchalant attitude towards gas attack that there are no records of the number of casualties.

---

21   Ibid., pp. 45–485, 'On the question of morality ... gas has been openly accepted as a recognised weapon for the future, and there is no longer any question of stealing an unfair advantage by taking an unsuspecting enemy unawares. Apart from this it has been pointed out that tribesmen are not bound by The Hague convention and they do not conform to most elementary rules ...'

It was not as if only the British were guilty of such crimes. France, Spain and other nations too used chemical weapons. The Geneva Protocol remained a bare skeleton and what remained of it was finally buried by Germany and Russia. The two countries entered a pact in 1928, under which they collaborated with Russia in a series of top secret tests called Project Tomka at a site in the Soviet Union about 20 km west of Volsk.

For the next five years, around thirty German experts lived and worked alongside a large number of Soviet staff mainly engaged in testing mustard gas. The entire project was top secret, and only a handful of Soviet government officials were aware of it. The security measures surrounding Project Tomka were such that any of its participants who spoke about it to outsiders risked capital punishment.

It may not have been a coincidence, but Japan too got into the fray the same year and started manufacturing mustard gas. They got into Lewisite production as well and were soon producing 2 tons of the chemical per week. Through extensive testing and trials on Formosa island in 1930, the Japanese developed an impressive array of gas weapons—rockets able to deliver 10 litres of agent up to 3 km; devices for emitting a 'gas fog'; flame-throwers modified to hurl jets of hydrogen cyanide; mustard spray bombs which released streams of gas while gently floating to earth, attached to parachutes; and remotely controlled contamination trailers capable of laying mustard in strips 7 m wide among others.

As if this wasn't enough, Japan set up the Army Chemical Warfare School for training soldiers in 1933 at Narashino, 34 km east of Tokyo. It had a 40-acre site and impressive facilities. The first commandant of the school was Major General Yamazaki. His singular focus was on training the cadets in combat, tactics and conducting chemical warfare, with the sole aim of winning wars. Within the next eleven years, the school turned out 3,350 trained chemical warfare experts. This was a clear testimony to the success of Major General Yamazaki's vision. The students were carefully selected officers who underwent the eleven-month course. They were bound by strict codes of conduct where they took an oath that human rights, human ethics and other hopeless values like compassion would not come in the way of their duties.[22]

At around the same time, Italy used 700 tons of chemical weapons in the invasion of Abyssinia,[23] under the guidance of dictator Benito Mussolini, with his grand dreams of expanding his reign. Several African countries were colonized by European nations at that time, and Mussolini's strategy was a part of the same plan. Once he had control over Abyssinia, Italy could dominate right up to Somalia. Moreover, these countries were easy prey for powerful nations. In October 1935, Mussolini attacked Abyssinia, putting forward the most frivolous reasons, and the war ended in May 1936. Abyssinia was so weak that it had no weapons to face Mussolini's ready army. Abyssinian Emperor Haile Selassie appealed to the youth of his country to join the fight against the Italians. Thousands of young men heeded his call and joined the army to fight for their motherland, armed with bows, arrows and spears. Mussolini was so cruel and impenitent that he bombarded the powerless Abyssinian army with chemical weapons. Winston Churchill and others went a step further and brazenly applauded these inhuman actions.

The Italians had made mustard gas bombs containing 200 pounds of the gas which they sprayed from planes flying at very low altitudes. The liquid lingered on the ground and on vegetation, contaminating not only troops but peasants passing through the area. The local correspondent of the *London Times* wrote a shocking

---

22 Ibid., pp. 50–51.

23 Ibid., pp. 52–53; David Nicolle and Raffaele Ruggeri, *The Italian Invasion of Abyssinia 1935–36*; A.J. Barker, *The Rape of Ethiopia 1936*.

and moving piece that bought the atrocities happening in Abyssinia to the world at large—at least fifteen thousand people died, and they were the fortunate ones.

Dr Robert Kelly was the head of the British Red Cross headquarters in Abyssinia, to which droves of blinded victims with untreated skin wounds infected with gangrene struggled their way to, many of them women, children and infants. Only death could deliver them from their unspeakable misery. This was certainly not war; this was manslaughter of the worst kind.

British Prime Minister Stanley Baldwin described the Italian use of mustard gas as a 'peril to the world', and he voiced the question on the minds of most of the world's governments: 'If a great European nation, in spite of having given its signature to the Geneva Protocol against the use of such gases, employs them in Africa, what guarantee have we that they may not be used in Europe?' But he didn't ban the use of chemical weapons by his country because the British intelligence agency MI3 reported that 'in a future war Italy would not hesitate to employ gas weapons against its own neighbours'.

Meanwhile, though the Second World War had not started as yet, war cries could be heard in the distance. Several European countries began feeling that soon enough they would have to be ready. Following reports of the atrocities Italy committed in Abyssinia and the MI3 warnings, the British government announced that everyone in the United Kingdom was to be issued with a gas mask and civilians would be trained on how to use it. Special masks were designed for babies, invalids and the elderly. Official government films warning of the dangers of poison gas were shown in cinemas; signboards on buses and underground trains encouraged citizens to carry their masks at all times.

While on one side British citizens were being trained in self-defence, countries were working on increasing their manufacturing capacity of chemical weapons in a systematic manner. The British too were aware that they needed a substantial chemical arsenal, and so they decided to set up a new mustard gas factory near Lancashire with the cooperation of Imperial Chemical Industries (ICI).[24] The cabinet ordered the creation of an industrial productive capacity of 300 tons of mustard gas per week, and a reserve of 2,000 tons.

France too joined the race and decided to increase its chemical weapon manufacturing capacity tremendously. A factory was set up at Clamency to produce phosgene, at a cost of almost 20 million francs.

Meanwhile, Russia set up new factories at Brandyuzhsky, Kuibyshev and Karaganda to increase its chemical weapon supplies. Germany had already entered a secret pact with the Soviet Russia and was collaborating with them in the search for newer chemical weapons. Once this was known to the other European countries, they were under increased pressure. They had some idea about what was happening in Germany, but no clue about what unfolded behind the veils of secrecy in communist Russia. Britain and France desperately tried to find out about Russia's efforts, but failed. Finally, France and Britain decided to joined hands, and Britain opened the doors of its chemical weapons facility at Porton for the French.

The French developed large, egg-shaped grenades filled with mustard gas to be dropped in clutches of fifty at a time. These had no fuses, and were designed to simply break on impact. The French shared this technology with Britain, and in return the British offered them a method for high-altitude spraying of mustard gas from a height of 15,000 feet, away from the danger of anti-aircraft guns. The two countries relied heavily on mustard gas, phosgene and each other.

---

24 Robert Harris and Jeremy Paxman, *A Higher Form of Killing*, pp. 52–54.

But none of this was going to prove fruitful, because Germany was doing something unprecedented. It had developed a chemical weapon that was going to outshine everything else. Around 1936, Germany was striving to add this extremely toxic, destructive chemical weapon to its arsenal. The Allies had some inkling about what was happening, but they couldn't get their hands on the formula for the new German weapon.

The new weapon was developed by Dr Gerhard Schrader, a German scientist researching possible new insecticides. While he was painstakingly working his way through an enormous range of organic phosphorus compounds, he stumbled upon a series of poisons of extraordinary power. On 23 December 1936, he managed to prepare the chemical for the first time, and tested it by spraying a concentration of just one part in 2,00,000 on some leaf lice. All the insects were killed. He found that small insects were killed within seconds, while larger animals like rats took about a minute to die. The chemical had an unbearably offensive smell.

An accident occurred during his research when the container with the chemical tilted and spilt in the laboratory. Dr Schrader lost his eyesight all of a sudden. There was no stinging pain like with the mustard gas and no peeling of the skin. Just darkness. His assistants and he struggled their way outside the lab where it was sunny. They could feel the sunlight on their eyes. The doctor noted that the chemical caused the power of sight to be weakened in artificial light. Just a few spilt drops had caused such a severe effect. What would it be like if it was used on a large scale?

This question prodded Dr Schrader to further his research. Direct research on humans would be too hazardous, and hence it was monkeys and dogs that had to bear the brunt. Almost a hundred dogs and monkeys were picked for the research, and large quantities of the new chemical were sprayed on their bodies. The effects showed within minutes. The animals lost muscular control; their pupils contracted so much that their eyes looked completely white. Their limbs began to twitch and jerk. Within fifteen minutes they convulsed and died.

The name sent a chill down the spine: nerve gas. Its commercial name was 'Tabun'.

Dr Schrader's curiosity was kindled even more. He got the support of Otto Ambros, Colonel Rudiger, who was heading Hitler's gas protection lab, and some others. They had to analyse these poisonous compounds, and based on their findings find ways of enhancing their toxicity.

Results showed that the nerve gas inhibited the action of cholinesterase in the body. Cholinesterase controls the muscles by breaking down the chemical which causes muscular contraction, acetylcholine. That is how we can move our limbs and muscles as much as we want. Dr Schrader's new chemical toxin interfered with the action of cholinesterase and increased its concentration in the body to such disastrous levels that all the muscles of the body would contract. The body thus poisoned itself and lost control of all its functions. The muscles of the arms and legs along with those which controlled respiration and defecation went into a state of violent vibration, resulting in death due to asphyxiation.

Once they had deciphered Tabun's effects, the four of them studied several organo-phosphorus compounds, isolated the effective ones and formulated them in controlled quantities. This effort was crucial because it was cumbersome and complicated to employ these as chemical weapons. They needed something that was fast-acting and easy to use. It was found soon enough.

This group developed isopropyl methylphosphonofluoridate, a chemical compound related to Tabun. Its potential as a toxic war substance was found to be astonishingly high. It was easy to use and was called sarin, a name invented by Schrader as an acronym of the names of the key individuals involved in its development—

Schrader, Ambros and Rudiger. Such a harmful and toxic chemical had never been developed before. Drunk on their success, the scientists informed Berlin about their invention. Senior officers of the German army tested it, and once its effectiveness and toxicity was confirmed, the news was passed on to Hitler himself in 1939.[25]

The Second World War had just begun, and Germany had invaded Poland when the scientists announced the development of the new chemical weapon. Three weeks after Poland had fallen, Hitler said while addressing a gathering in Danzig on 19 September 1939: 'Our enemies should not underestimate our strength. Even if all nations come together, they will not be able to save themselves; because the Germans have a formidable weapon on their hands for which no one has an answer as yet.'

It is possible that he was speaking about the new nerve gas. At that time, no one else had a clue about what it could do. His announcement was followed by an order to the German chemical industry to build a new factory capable of producing 1,000 tons of Tabun a month. Several big names invested their money in this project. Since the post-First World War scenario wasn't very clear, the established companies maintained an arm's length from the new entity. This led to the building of the secret but massive factory close to the Oder River, 40 km from Breslau, at a place called Dyhernfurth. It was built on a mile-long and half-a-mile-wide plot with six factories capable of producing 500 tons of poison gas, adding up to 3,000 tons a month. Hitler planned to turn it into Europe's largest chlorine factory after Germany won the war. The factory was completely self-contained at that time, producing all the intermediates needed for the manufacture of nerve gas and Tabun. It had a cavernous underground shell-filling plant, where the liquid nerve gas was loaded into aircraft bombs and shells. Altogether, the

---

25   Ibid., pp. 55–58.

factory employed an all-German workforce of 3,000 working day and night.

It took over two years—until April 1942—to get the factory operational to full capacity because many of the chemicals needed to make the liquid nerve gases were exceptionally corrosive and all iron and steel equipment had to be plated with silver to avoid rusting and corrosion. The nerve gas itself was so toxic that the entire plant had to be enclosed in double-glass-lined chambers with pressurized air circulating between the layers; all apparatus had to be decontaminated with steam and ammonia.

It was a huge challenge to keep the workers safe. They wore respirators and special protective suits made of cloth sandwiched between two layers of rubber, which were burnt after every tenth use. Even before production got underway at the factory, there were over 300 accidents. In the two and a half years that it was operational, at least ten men were killed. Four pipe-fitters died when a large quantity of Tabun drained on to them from pipes they were trying to clean. They went into a state of convulsion before their rubber suits could be torn off. Some with mild symptoms could be easily recognized by their contracted pupils.

The elaborate safety precautions cost a lot of money and almost 120 million Deutsche marks were spent on these factories. Apart from these, the Germans had a score of factories capable of producing around 12,000 tons of poison gas every month. In addition to Tabun, the Germans had two types of mustard gas and a terrifying incendiary gas, N-Stoff (chlorine trifluoride), which could cause clothes, hair and even asphalt to burst into flames even in freezing temperatures. Germany was simultaneously developing novel ways of using these chemical weapons. One method was to fill small, delicate containers with mustard gas and bury them in holes in the ground. The containers would burst whenever anyone stepped on them. In another method, they filled a large number of empty lightbulbs with mustard gas and buried them in the ground. When heavy trucks or tanks rolled over them, the bulbs burst, releasing large quantities of the gas.

The Germans tested a machine gun capable of firing 2,000 rounds of ammunition charged with tabun or sarin per minute. There were hand grenades filled with cyanide and gas grenades that could be used as anti-tank weapons. A huge cache of 5,000 such bombs had been accumulated. Apart from these, they had mechanized spray guns that could spray large quantities of gas on advancing enemy soldiers. All these had been duly tested. Hitler had a good idea about the devastation these chemical weapons could cause on the battlefield, killing not only animals but even human beings to prove it.

All these weapons were ready to be used. The only question left to be answered was what response the Allies would have. What if they had something more powerful? These questions festered in Hitler's mind. He decided against using these chemical weapons till answers were found. He hadn't forgotten that he himself was once wounded by nerve gas in the First World War and had almost gone blind.

However, he couldn't handle the pressure for too long because the war was in progress and the scales were fast tilting towards the Allies. There was tremendous pressure on Hitler to use chemical weapons. Three of the most fanatical Nazi leaders, Martin Bormann, Joseph Goebbels and Robert Ley, repeatedly urged Hitler to unleash the nerve gas.

1944 dawned and Hitler was in a dilemma. D-Day at Normandy had just passed on 6 June, and the Germans had faced an embarrassing defeat there. The only option that remained was to use chemical weapons and poison gas bombs. Finally, the Nazi commanders ordered the chemical weapons be kept ready for attack. They had been waiting for that moment and did not waste a moment following Hitler's orders. They were in a hurry and were happily visualizing the devastation their powerful chemical weapons could cause. Their dreams were about to come true. The Germans went ahead and rolled out stocks of tabun and other toxins from the secret locations in the Bavarian jungles. The last chapter of the Second World War had begun.

5

The Darkness of Intoxication in Japan

THERE are two distinct opinions that come up whenever Japan is mentioned. The first is how much the country had to endure; and the second, how it rose like a phoenix despite being razed to the ground. There are no doubts about the latter, but the collective social sympathy on the former is misplaced.

While Germany was crossing several milestones in chemical warfare, Japan was scaling new heights in the field of biological warfare. Some Japanese generals revelled in watching human beings die, and developed newer ways of killing people. It can be asserted that the Japanese scientists' behaviour was equally cruel, if not more, than that of Hitler.

If ever the history of human barbarity and savagery is documented, several chapters would be dedicated to Japan, alongside Germany. Japan's tumultuous relationship with its neighbour, China, goes back as far as the sixth century.[26] Even in those days, the bone of contention between the two countries were Taiwan and Korea. The two nations had fought a war in 670 AD. The same conflict has been continuing for the last 150 years, and opium stands at the centre of this dispute. Britain, and later Japan, encouraged China to grow opium, which was banned in the US and Britain. But these two countries, along with Spain, Holland and other smaller nations, heavily invested in opium trade. The East India Company got a monopoly in opium cultivation in India in 1761, when opium auctions would take place in Calcutta. Many Parsi and Gujarati traders were involved in the business. Since the sale of opium was banned in many countries, the focus was on the Chinese market. But China was not interested in any kind of global business. Its rulers held an iron grip on the economy and were suspicious of all foreigners. The British were the first ones to knock on the closed doors of the Chinese market. They succeeded after a lot of effort and persistence and got permission for international trade from the port at Guangzhou, known as Canton then. Once they found a foothold, they took over.

In 1773, England brought opium into China, and soon the Chinese economy went into a tailspin. According to records, the Chinese government had 26 lakh tons of silver stock, but in the following twenty-seven years, by 1820, it had slipped to around 8 tons. By 1900, only the hollow shell of glorious Chinese history remained. Over a crore people had become addicted to opium and the drug had tightened its grip right on the royal family, the army, the government and the common man. Though China was a massive country, it was torn apart by internal disharmony and friction. The powerful countries of the world took advantage of the situation and

---

26 BBC, 'China and Japan: Rival Giants and Rape of Nanjing', 17 June 2011.

pushed China into the abyss of addiction. The rulers of the hollow country were equally clueless.

In 1894, Japan attacked the depleted Qing dynasty and captured Taiwan. It also took a commitment from China for opening up three Korean ports for trade. Glenn Melancon, author of *Britain's China Crisis and the Opium Crisis*, and Hunt Janin, author of *The India–China Opium Trade in the Nineteenth Century*, have shown that money from the opium trade was behind the Industrial Revolution and economic prosperity. Quite a few books have been written describing in detail how prosperous and developed Asia was before the entry of the British. The huge amounts of capital needed for England's industrial development came from the sale of opium.

Japan and a handful of other nations were behind the cultivation of opium in China. Japan fought almost eleven wars in this area, one of them for the occupation of Korea. Japan ruled over Korea for thirty-six years and encouraged the cultivation of opium there as well, ruining the local administration.

Japan's ambitions began growing, and it fought a war with the Russian empire in 1904 over Chinese territories. The war went on for one and a half years and finally ended with a treaty at Portsmouth. According to the treaty, Russia's ownership over China was nullified and Japan was given control over the Chinese territory of Manchuria.

The historical coincidence was such that this treaty was signed under the aegis of US President Theodore Roosevelt, the first cousin of Franklin Roosevelt, who became US President in 1933. Japan was emboldened with the US's apparent partiality, and further strengthened by China's weakened Qing dynasty that had become hollow because of opium addiction. 1912 marked the end of imperial rule and the formation of the Chinese Republic, but it wasn't going to cause any dramatic improvement in the situation. The erstwhile ruling families had disintegrated, but their chips remained. The central government was yet to hold sway, and a lot of powerful regional satraps came up and began joining hands with each other. Manchurian leader Zhang Zuolin was one of those who built connections with Japan.

Owing to the rise of such regional leaders and the circumstances in China, Japan was becoming progressively audacious and was constantly on the lookout for a reason to attack it. Just when the First World War was coming to a close, Japan attacked China's Shandong province. It wanted Shandong and Manchuria to strengthen the Japanese economy. Hence, Japan trained its eyes on these regions and constantly tried to capture them. In 1930, Japan became emboldened by the public uprising in China and its intrusions increased manifold. The Chinese government was hardly able to handle its internal problems and was not in a position to focus on Japan's ulterior motives. Finally, on 19 September 1931, the Japanese army attacked Manchuria and tried to capture its cities. After striving for five months, it had control over the province. Manchuria was important for Japan's sovereignty; it was renamed Manchukuo. Puyi, the last emperor of China, was appointed the puppet head of Manchukuo.

Most people wouldn't be aware that Japan desired to make Manchukuo like the Israel of old. Under a strategy known as the Fugu Plan, Japan wanted to rope in Jews from Europe to settle in Manchukuo. (Fugu is an extremely poisonous but delicious kind of puffer fish that is popular among the rich in Japan. Eating it can prove fatal if it is not cooked properly. The plan was named after this fish—appealing but dangerous.[27]) Japan had a two-pronged strategy. The first reasoning was that this would make separating the province from China easy, and the second that they could get a lot of aid from the US. Japan put forth this plan to the Jews and

---

27 Marvin Tokayer and Mary Swartz, *The Fugu Plan: The Untold Story of the Japanese and the Jews during World War II*.

rained sops and discounts on them with the intention of garnering a lot of financial and technical knowledge. According to the plan, on one side they were inviting Jews to come to Manchukuo, and on the other cultivating opium on a large scale.[28]

Japan later took over the production of heroin from opium and its supply to Western countries, with the cooperation of some well-known Japanese corporations of today.[29] Japan soon became the world's largest producer of opium thanks to these companies. But the Fugu Plan did not succeed. Japan had hoped that a large number of Jews would come from Russia and Germany, but Russia signed a friendship pact with Germany and the road for the Jews was closed for good.

Despite the failure of the Fugu Plan, opium cultivation was in full bloom! Close to the end of the First World War, Japan alone was exporting 20 tons of morphine and heroin to China. It soon became the world's largest opium producer. Later, in 1937, the League of Nations' International Narcotics Control Bureau blamed Japan for the abundance of opium and pronounced that it was responsible for spreading opium addiction worldwide.

But this was much later. China was helpless at that time and didn't have the military might to take on the Japanese, or any friends to come to their aid. In desperation, it registered a complaint against Japan in the United Nations, which had come into being soon after the First World War. It made inquiries and pronounced Japan guilty. Japan was expelled from the UN, but its aggression didn't stop. China and Japan fought a war yet again in January 1932, with

---

28   Marvin Tokayer and Mary Swartz, *The Fugu Plan: The Untold Story of the Japanese and the Jews during World War II.*

29   John M. Jennings, *The Opium Empire: Japanese Imperialism and Drug Trafficking in Asia, 1895–1945.*

Shanghai being the battleground this time around.[30] Japan captured this important Chinese city, and the very next year seized the area surrounding the Great Wall. Meanwhile, Japan was also trying to drive a wedge between the nationalist government that had come to power in the Nanjing province and the Manchukuo province that it had captured. It took full advantage of the misunderstandings that had cropped up between the two. Even though the Second World War had begun in Europe, there was no end to the strife between China and Japan. Japan was not letting go of a single opportunity to squeeze China. An integral part of its strategy was biological warfare.

One morning at 5 a.m., Japan flew a small plane over Hunan in China. The usual sirens blared and people rushed to hide. They covered their ears in anticipation of a loud blast, but there was none. The plane just hovered and flew back. There were no bombs dropped, but what fell from the plane was bird feed that the chickens and ducks ate: corn and millets. The Chinese found it amusing, and some of them picked up the seeds, which stuck to their palms, but they thought nothing of it.

The next day, the hens and ducks began dropping dead, as if struck by an epidemic. The attack was so severe that the entire Hunan province had no hens or ducks for a while.

The same fate was seen in neighbouring areas, but the difference was that small, egg-like objects were dropped instead of grains. The egg-like objects that fell in water swelled up like a sponge. Once they reached their capacity, they burst and a sticky fluid oozed out. Within a few days, the number of rats in the area increased. Soon, people noticed swellings in their armpits and thighs. Within days, the plague had spread throughout the province.

In a few other places, the Japanese sprayed poison on to water bodies, causing diarrhoea to spread. People had severe loose motions

---

30 Jeanne Guillemin, *Biological Weapons*, pp. 80–85.

which led to death. In another province, the Japanese spread glanders-causing micro-organisms, which had no effect on any part of the body except the legs, causing them to decay steadily.

But even this wasn't enough for Japan, which was doing everything by trial and error, without concrete scientific evidence. To that end, it set up an independent laboratory referred to as the epidemic prevention and water filtration department, but it was only a front. Under it, three laboratories were established in Shenyang, Chang Chun and Ping Fan provinces of China. The headquarters was known as Unit 731. It had laboratories spread over 150 buildings, two underground prisons, and a cemetery attached to each unit to deal with those who lost their lives in the experiments. The construction of these units started, and the doctors began their work around 1939. The more we read about their despicable deeds, the more ashamed we feel about the human race.[31]

Most of the experiments were done on Chinese prisoners. Occasionally, Russians were used but the primary guinea pigs were predominantly Chinese. Initial participants in the experiments had germs of typhoid, cholera, plague, etc. injected into them. Once they got infected, the bodies of the living men were opened up to see how the germs were working in the body. This process is called vivisection, where the victim's body is cut up without any anesthesia, purely for experimental studies. For example, if a prisoner had been exposed to cholera-causing bacteria, his stomach would be taken apart to identify the exact point at which his digestive system failed. In one instance, the abdomen of a living pregnant woman was opened up. She screamed and wailed in pain, and after some time lost consciousness. As she was taking her last breath, she came to her

---

31   Robert Harris and Jeremy Paxman, *A Higher Form of Killing*, pp. 50–51.

senses for a brief moment. All she could say was, 'Please spare the life of my baby.'

In one experiment involving the study of the limits to which humans can tolerate lowered atmospheric pressure, a group of prisoners was kept in a sealed room, and the pressure was gradually reduced. At one point, the pressure became so low that their eyes popped out of their sockets like soda-bottle corks and blood spouted from their ears!

In another experiment, doctors severed both hands of a prisoner and grafted the right hand to the left shoulder, and vice versa. As if this wasn't enough, they interchanged his legs as well. They wanted to study how the human brain's command mechanism worked!

In some tests, a healthy prisoner would be tied to an infected prisoner to study the time taken for the infection to spread. Sometimes, horse's blood or plain air was injected into a person's veins. The air would form intravenous bubbles and prove fatal. Some prisoners were given drips of sea water to study if it could be an alternative to medicinal saline. Couples were selected and either the husband or the wife was infected with venereal disease-causing germs. They would be observed during intercourse and the exact process of transmission recorded.

Some experiments were also said to have been conducted on three- or four-year-old children. To study the amount of blood loss required to cause death, large gaping wounds were made on a person's body and they were allowed to bleed to death. There were other experiments that were even more inhuman! In one, prisoners were tied to centrifuges that were like merry-go-rounds and spun around. The speed was increased till all the prisoners died. If a few survived, the spinning continued till they too died. Once the dead bodies were brought down, there would be bleeding from the eye sockets, nose and ears. The experiment was to check the speed and time needed to cause death.

The next class of experiments was designed with the purpose of creating bombs with disease-causing germs. People were intentionally infected with plague and other organisms, and the rats and flies that came in contact with the infected people were caught and bred to increase their numbers. Such infected animals and insects were later used as bombs—around 4 lakh Chinese citizens were exterminated in this way.

Dr Kurumizawa Masakuni was among those who conducted these experiments, testified after his arrest and spilled the beans about all the activities of Unit 731. Till then, the world did not know the details of the goings-on there. Another member of the same unit was arrested and he too confessed and broke down in front of the police. Even after so many years, we are shaken reading one of his accounts, 'My hands trembled while cutting open a living human being for the first time, but I got used to it. There was a procedure where we would tell ourselves that there was a log of wood on the table and not a human being. And the prisoners too were numbered as log 1, 2, 3 … and so on.' He added, 'Despite having so much practice, my hands began sweating at one time and I felt giddy because the log I had to cut that day was a person I knew well and was very close to … but I could do nothing … I cut open his chest with the knife I held. I can never forget in my life, the look of hatred I saw in his eyes.'

'What did I do?' he said and cried uncontrollably.

Despite knowing how heinous and atrocious all these methods were, why didn't those in charge stop them?

That was because Emperor Hirohito and the royal family looked the other way when it came to Japan's biological warfare.[32] All official permissions required for the inhuman experiments were given by the emperor himself. Prince Kotohito and General Sugiyama were

---

32   Jeanne Guillemin, *Biological Weapons*, pp. 79–87.

responsible for ensuring that the royal commands were followed, and the atrocities committed as per expectations.[33] Japan, however, has rejected all these accusations.

The main aim of the unit was to produce biological weapons of mass destruction. Plague, typhoid, cholera and many such germ bombs were produced here. Japan wanted to get this biological arsenal ready for use in the Second World War. Almost 300 kg plague germs, 550 kg anthrax, 900 kg of typhoid and 1,000 kg of cholera and other biological weapons were produced in the three centres put together. The raw material for these was the flesh and blood of 11,000 Chinese, Korean and Russian prisoners.

Unit 731 fell directly under the control of the royal police. There were several centres working on the production of biological weapons and chemical weapons in the Japanese defence establishment. Unit 531 and Unit 543 were in Hailar, while Unit 773 was in Songo. Unit 100 was operative in Changchun, Unit 1644 in Nanking and Unit 1855 in Beijing. The unit that functioned in Singapore was 9420. All these units were managed and coordinated by Unit 731.

The charge of all these units rested with General Shiro Ishii,[34] a physician and microbiologist by profession. Born in 1892 in Shibayama village, he studied medicine in Kyoto Imperial University and was well-known as a supremely brilliant student. He was as selfish as he was ambitious. In 1922, he joined the medical corps of the Japanese army and rose up the ranks fast. He got a chance to go on a two-year tour of the West in 1928, where he did extensive research on the effects of biological warfare and chemical warfare

---

33   Herbert P. Bix, *Hirohito and the Making of Modern Japan*.

34   Yuki Tanaka, *Hidden Horrors: Japanese War Crimes in World War II*, p. 138; Daniel Barenblatt, *A Plague Upon Humanity: The Secret Genocide of Axis Japan's Germ Warfare Operation*, p. 173; Robert Harris and Jeremy Paxman, *A Higher Form of Killing*, p. 143.

from the First World War I onwards. He got deeply interested in the field of biological warfare.

On his return, Ishii met the minister for the Japanese army, Sadao Araki, and told him about what he had learnt on his tour, presenting a vision and plan of doing something similar in Japan. Araki was extremely pleased, and he informed Emperor Hirohito about Ishii's plans. The emperor was so impressed that he instantly gave his nod for the project, and the first such centre came into being in 1932. Ishii was given full, formal control of it by Emperor Hirihito and Minister Araki. He proved equal to the task, and with a chosen handful of officers set up a first-of-its-kind high-security prison/experimentation camp in Zhongma, a small village 100 km south of Manchuria. It was more like a fortress where a special group called the Togo unit was assembled under Ishii's leadership. The other members were Lt Col. Ryoichi Naito, Major General Dr Masaji Kitano, Yoshio Shinozuka, Yasuji Kaneko and others— all senior government officers, microbiology professors and the like. They immediately got working on their experiments, beginning with conducting tests on a handful of prisoners. Once they were convinced they could conduct experiments on a large scale, they expanded the scope of their work. What followed was the setting up of an independent facility for which Emperor Hirohito gave his authorization in writing and where Ishii had complete autonomy and supremacy. Soon, several such experimentation units were set up and collectively called by the misleading name of Epidemic Prevention and Water Purification Department of the Kwantung Army—also known as Unit 731 in short.

The security initiatives of the unit were code-named 'maruta'. Initially, the living subjects for the experiments were people picked up from nearby jungles—called 'logs'. For example, 'Today we found forty logs.' Over time, jailed prisoners, small-time thieves and political prisoners formed a steady flow of subjects to the unit.

A list of rebels who were potential threats to Emperor Hirohito was readied. It had old women and even small children on it, and served only as a means to provide a steady stream of subjects for the unit. Whoever went in would not come out alive.

The Unit 731 headquarters had been designed in military style, spread over an area of 6 square km, consisting of 150 buildings. The ones that contained the labs were bomb-proof. They had 4,500 underground tanks made of high-quality cast iron that were bomb-proof and fire-proof. There were six gigantic trenches made of cement and concrete used for the production of biological bombs. Some of those buildings exist even to this day and are open to tourists. They have been converted and preserved as memorials of the wars.

An important sub-division of this unit was in Hiroshima, where the production of high-quality chemical weapons for the Japanese army was done. Huge quantities of mustard gas, Lewisite, etc., were produced here. This unit was so secret that the area was not shown on official maps. The answer to the question of why the US dropped the atomic bomb on Hiroshima during the Second World War can be found here. This division had mobile units, the head of which was Ishii's close friend. Workers in these units would travel to villages in the guise of vaccine administrators, wearing white coats like doctors. They would inject unsuspecting villagers with disease-causing germs.

This division was active throughout the Second World War, and produced massive quantities of chemical and biological weapons. Emperor Hirohito and Ishii were very keen to see these employed on the battlefield, but were delayed by some last-minute glitch or the other.

On 7 December 1941, Japan attacked Pearl Harbor and gave the US a rude shock. In that surprise operation, the Japanese navy stealthily reached the harbour and destroyed all the fuel supplies stored there—a huge embarrassment for the superpower in the making. President Franklin Roosevelt was peeved and desperately wanted to teach Japan a lesson.

He made a supremely bold plan of attack referred to as the 'Tokyo Raid' or 'Dolittle Raid'. It was planned, led by and named after Lt Colonel James Doolittle. There isn't much talk about it but it was an important military operation; a one-sided campaign where the participants were clearly told, 'It is all right if you don't make it back, but Tokyo must be destroyed.' As a matter of fact, no one was expected to make it back alive. The crew had been instructed, 'Keep bombing till you have life left in you and keep flying till the planes have fuel in the tanks. When the fuel begins to get exhausted, fly to China and crash the airplanes wherever possible. If you survive; well and good, or else its goodbye!'

Aircraft carrier USS Hornet, loaded with 16 B-25 bomber aircrafts, docked as close to Tokyo as possible. Once the orders were received, they flew over Tokyo, Yokohama, Osaka and Nagoya and rained bombs for as long as fuel remained in the tanks. There was no way the planes could return to base, so they flew into China with the bare minimum fuel remaining. Some got destroyed, while a few managed to reach the airbase at Zhuzhou, where local Chinese residents came to the crew's help and hid them in their village.

For the first time, Japan got a taste of what war was like. Senior Japanese army officials couldn't in their wildest dreams have imagined an attack of such massive proportions. Japan was totally shaken and Emperor Hirohito was crazed. He had to do something to avenge the humiliation, and he found an easy way: China. The imperial army took out its fury on the Chinese people, conducting 600 air raids on the village that gave refuge to US airplanes.

In an operation code-named 'Sei-go', Japanese soldiers picked up local Chinese people one by one and killed them. Ishii's biological weapons came in handy; seven bio-bombs were dropped on the Zhejiang province. The civilians who survived the germ attack were rolled in cloth soaked in kerosene, and lit by matches held by close relatives. Many women had to burn their own husbands and then be subjected to the assault of Japanese soldiers. The fire of revenge was so intense and perverse that the soldiers went to the extent of chopping off women's breasts. Two and a half lakh people perished in this quest for vengeance, but it was not enough to quell Japan's anger. In the three months that followed, a further two to three lakh people died due to chemical and biological weapons, 50,000 of plague alone.

Meanwhile, the Second World War was gathering momentum, and Japan had become a prime player. The quest to use biological weapons had to be put on hold after the Russians invaded the Manchukuo and Mengjiang provinces. Once the pressure from Russia increased and the direction of the war became evident, Ishii had to ask his employees to leave. They had all been given potassium cyanide ampoules and instructed to use them if they were caught. On Ishii's orders, the Japanese army dug new underground tunnels and began destroying their biological weapon-manufacturing units to avoid them from falling into enemy hands.

In 1945, Japan had to surrender, and General Douglas MacArthur, who was extolled for his military leadership of the US, was given the reins.[35] It was now clear that Ishii's time was up because lawsuits were filed against the Nazis who committed atrocities on the Jews.

---

35   Ibid., p. 155, Jeanne Guillemin, *Biological Weapons*, pp. 16, 76–78, 88–91. See, Chapter 4: 'Secret Sharing and the Japanese Biological Weapons Program'; United States Responses to Japanese Wartime Inhuman Experimentation after World War II: National Security and Wartime Exigency, 'The final report by U.S. scientists from Camp Detrick was submitted in December 1947, by technical director Dr Edwin V. Hill and staff pathologist Dr Joseph Victor. Ishii's group now gave the Americans detailed reports on the experimental program, including a listing of 8000 pathological slides and hundreds of color drawings', National Library of Medicine.

A special court was set up in Nuremburg and some Japanese too had to be present there. Cases were filed in courts in Tokyo as well.

However, nothing came out of it. While the case was on, General MacArthur sent a telegram to Washington: 'Don't touch Ishii. Pardon him.' The case was reported later as 'Materials on the Trial of Former Servicemen of the Japanese Army Charged with Manufacturing and Employing Bacteriological Weapons'. The Russians took copies of the same in as many languages as possible. This report had every single detail of the inhuman cruelties that Ishii and his colleagues had committed. But despite all this, nobody could touch him. Actually, the judgment that was passed against the killers of the Jews and the perpetrators of crimes in Auschwitz should have been given for this Japanese criminal as well, but the US pardoned him. And all this for the sole reason that Ishii had agreed to give the US all the secret documents related to the manufacture of biological bombs and chemical weapons!

This fact is as true as it is frightening. It is an indication of how hypocritical the world and its superpowers are and the kind of double games they play. According to later reports, Emperor Hirohito's Japan had killed many Jews[36] but made to suffer no consequences! Every single person responsible for the Auschwitz concentration camp was convicted and punished but Unit 731, even worse compared to the atrocities of Auschwitz, was allowed to go scot-free. This was because Japan had agreed to accept US supremacy. Ishii was not punished for his heinous crimes and was instead appointed as a professor at the University of Maryland.

He taught the intricacies of biological weapons manufacture and continued to conduct extensive research. Not only that, his colleague Dr Masaji Kitano, who had a major role to play in the development

---

36   Bernard Wasserstein, *Secret War in Shanghai: An Untold Story of Espionage, Intrigue, and Treason in World War II.*

of biological weapons along with Shiro Isshi, went on to become the head of the Tokyo unit of the Japanese pharmaceutical giant Green Cross. He too received official recognition from both the Japanese and US governments. Even otherwise, a lot of people worked in pharmaceutical and chemical companies with their heads held high. No cognizance of the Chinese victims was taken; they received hardly a fraction of the compensation that the Jews got.

Can we imagine what would happen if the present German government brought back Hitler's swastika symbolism and practices? Countries like the US, Israel and others would come together to form an alliance, put pressure, create a ruckus and not let it go ahead.

Japan did exactly that, but the world, and especially the US, didn't say a word. In August 1999, the Japanese Parliament passed a resolution with a majority of 166 to 71, according to which the flag of Unit 731 and its related organizations would be revived. The man responsible for the inhuman massacre, Emperor Hirohito, was venerated. Historians raised the question, 'How would the world react if Hitler was given divine stature?'

Forget getting answers, the people who had to take cognizance of it turned a blind eye. One section from the US went on to say that there wasn't enough evidence against Japan. But that proved to be untrue because, in August 2005, Japanese professor Dr Keiichi Tsuneishi ransacked the US war office, compiled information and exposed to the world that the parties involved in the manufacture of biological weapons received generous help from the US. People like Ishii and his colleagues received large amounts of money and gifts and were given important professional positions.

The US had been eyeing the research Japan had done in this area. It needed the technology and ownership for the manufacture of these bioweapons and germ warfare techniques to sustain and preserve its superpower status.

It was going to get it on a platter from Japan. But in the blink of an eye, another branch of this knowledge began growing in the backyard of a different prospective superpower: Soviet Russia. The shadow of this poison tree was going to eclipse a lot of people.

6

Black Islands, Red Lights

IN a way, we are fortunate that Hitler missed his target completely. In June 1944, he could have won the D-Day battle of Normandy. If that had happened, the face of the Second World War and the post-war world would have changed irreversibly.

The Allies were deeply frightened by the chemical weapons that Hitler possessed and weren't even sure exactly what kind they were or where they were stored. However, one section of the Allies believed that the fears were unfounded and Hitler actually had no chemical weapons other than those that had already been deployed. They were so certain that while preparing for the battle of Normandy, not a single soldier was equipped with protective gear against chemical warfare. General Montgomery left behind all the anti-gas equipment meant for the troops in England. If Hitler had used the lethal chemical gases tabun or sarin, the Allied soldiers would have had no escape. When the attack succeeded without much struggle and the result was in favour of the Allies, General Omar Bradley wrote, 'When D-Day finally ended … without a whiff of gas, I was vastly relieved.

For even a light sprinkling of persistent gas on Omaha Beach would have cost us our footing there.' General Bradley's opinion was that it was their good fortune that Hitler chose not to employ chemical weapons in Normandy.

Bradley was one of the US's senior-most military officers, commanding the First United States Army division during the invasion of Normandy. He was captain of the gigantic cruiser USS *Augusta* that carried the Allied soldiers who landed at Utah and Omaha Beach. His name features in the honours' list of those responsible for the Allied victory over Hitler. George Patton, the well-known general during the Second World War, after whom the Patton tanks are named, was Omar Bradley's colleague. Later, General Bradley expressed his criticism of Douglas MacArthur's war policies and these were taken seriously, showing his influence and power! General Bradley is counted among the top five-star generals of the U S army. Gas, in Bradley's view, could have 'forced a decision in one of history's climactic battles'. And his views carried a lot of weight.

If Hitler had used new weapons, the war would have stretched on for a minimum of six months, which England could not have withstood. In such a case, it would have given up, and the absence of a strong second front would have made it difficult for Russia's Stalin to impel the battle forward. According to a lot of war strategists, Stalin would have signed yet another friendship treaty with Hitler and got away. All this meant that had Hitler employed chemical weapons, the result of the war would have been completely different.

Actually, there were two reasons why Hitler's estimate went wrong.[37] The way the Allies were clueless about the kind of weapons the Germans possessed, Hitler too was equally in the dark about the Allies' chemical armory. He felt that the Allies would have more

---

37   Robert Harris and Jeremy Paxman, *A Higher Form of Killing*, p. 54.

dangerous chemical weapons compared to what Germany owned and was afraid of the consequences. It seems hard to imagine Hitler in a state of uncertainty, but he had a reason to think the way he did. Just a year before, after suffering a big blow from Russia, Hitler summoned two of his trusted associates, Albert Speer, and Otto Ambros, chemical warfare expert, to his base at Wolfsschanze.[38] (Speer was an architect who built the Nuremberg stadium and several German government buildings. His vision was to rebuild the entire city of Berlin after the war. Since he was a member of Hitler's inner circle, he was appointed the head of the armaments production unit of the army. He was one of those who apologized during the post-war Nuremberg trials. His book *Inside the Third Reich* is still popular.[39] Ambros was a chemist holding a senior position in the chemical giant company BASF. He was later a member of the research team of IG Farben, a company that manufactured chemical weapons and gases. He then became the head of Hitler's chemical weapons department. He was the one who informed Hitler about the effects of the deadly chemicals tabun and sarin in 1944. He was convicted after the war trial and sentenced to six years in prison.)

Wolfsschanze was Adolf Hitler's first eastern front military headquarters in the Second World War. The top-secret, high-security site was built about 8 km east of the small East Prussian town of Rastenburg. Hitler came here for the first time on 23 June 1941, and left for the last time on 20 November 1944. A deep bunker was dug underground and the roof was built by pouring molten iron. It was 6.5 square km wide, almost like a mini village. There were 2,000 people residing there. The bunker had about forty rooms, of which twenty were occupied by Hitler himself. When the war was at its peak, Hitler would finish the day's work and either watch movies, listen to

---

38   Ibid., pp. 65, 66.

39   Albert Speer, *Inside the Third Reich*.

Beethoven symphonies or Wagner's operas with his associates. (This was the same bunker where there was an assassination attempt on Hitler on 20 July 1944. The conspirators were hanged on the same day. This underground settlement was so strong that after the Allied victory in the Second World War, they had to explode several bombs to destroy it.) It was in the same bunker that Hitler consulted his close aides Speer and Ambros on the possibility of using chemical weapons to stop Russia in its tracks. He felt that they had no other option. Listening to Hitler's opinion, Ambros said, 'If we do this, even we have to bear the brunt of similar weapons ... even the Allies have chemical weapons!' Hitler responded, 'But we have chemical weapons like tabun and sarin, which no one else does. Nobody knows how to protect oneself from these weapons.'

Hitler had expected them to welcome his suggestion but he turned out to be wrong. Ambros said, 'There is no reason to believe that we are the only ones who possess these weapons. Many other nations have been researching on developing similar lethal chemical weapons and to believe that they haven't had success would be foolhardy.' Hitler, who envisaged controlling the world, lost his patience listening to Ambros and stomped out of the room in anger. However, he never could gather the courage to use his chemical arsenal after Ambros's caution and his own near-blindness during the First World War.

This was an error. In fact, the one thing that would have proved fatal for the Allies was their ineffective and hollow intelligence service. For almost eight years, not one of the powerful nations had received a clue about the chemical weapons Hitler possessed. By the time they got to know, the war had ended and the Allies had won. Despite that, they were shaken thinking about the consequences they would have faced had Hitler chosen to employ chemical weapons.

The two main challenges for Hitler were manufacturing the weapons and keeping them secret from the Allies—he was successful on both accounts. To keep them under wraps, Hitler and his associates had to keep changing their code names. Tabun was initially known as 'Le 100', then as 'Gelan', then as 'Substance 83'. Sarin was initially code-named 'Stoff 146', then 'Trilon 83' and 'Trilon 146' after a common German detergent.

All the chemicals needed in the manufacture of nerve gas were transported under false names. Several times, the raw materials would start their journeys with one name, and this would change almost three times by the time they arrived at their destination. Only Hitler and a few of his handpicked colleagues were aware of these names. He was so paranoid that even the most senior Nazi officials believed 'ignorance is bliss' because more information meant more problems. All the details about the chemical weapons were recorded in cipher in the so-called 'Black Book'—a volume the size of a warehouse ledger, an inch and a half thick. After the war, the Allies tried their best to get their hands on it, but the Nazi officials had burnt the book, burying the secrets forever! This was Hitler's biggest triumph.

Since 1939, the US and Britain had used every possible means via their intelligence services to gain knowledge of these secrets. At a joint meeting, US officials said, 'Stories of the German nerve gases have had such wide circulation from so many sources, some of which appear to be reliable, that it is believed that the Germans do have some gas which can be used in this manner.' But they did not know exactly what these were at that time.

The intelligence coup which finally convinced the Allies of the real dangers came two years later. On 11 May 1943, the British army in Tunisia captured an important German prisoner. The man—whose name does not appear in official records—was a chemist from the main Nazi chemical warfare laboratory at Spandau. Britain was able to gather sketchy details about Hitler's lethal chemical arsenal from the prisoner, who told them, 'They have created a clear, colorless liquid with little smell' which 'cannot be classed with any of the other war gases as it is a nerve poison', causing the eyes to shrink 'to a pin-head and asthma-like difficulties in breathing. In any heavier concentrations death occurs in about a quarter of an hour.' He added, 'When engaged on research work on these chemicals, he was under continued treatment ... One chemist lost his life in spite of constant injections of Lobelin to excite the respiratory centre. Tests with this gas are extremely dangerous as there is no perceptible threshold of irritation, as is the case with other gases ... by the time one is aware of the gas through its physiological effects [the only means of detection] it is too late ... We have named it "Trilon 83".'[40]

The prisoner passed on details of the chemicals involved in its manufacture, along with advice on defensive measures. All his information, advised the report, 'may be classified as reliable'. Only twenty-five copies were produced and circulated throughout Whitehall and Porton. Astonishingly, no cognizance was taken. Another instance of the British carelessness was when they found a potent chemical similar to what Hitler possessed while working on DDT, but ignored it, realizing its importance only in April 1945, close to the end of the Second World War. The British had confiscated a truckload of German cannon balls and analysed one of them with the help of US experts, finding that it was Hitler's deadly weapon. It hit them hard when they realized that they themselves could have developed it easily. One of the scientists at the Porton chemical laboratory commented on the humiliation, saying, 'We got caught with our pants down.'[41]

Despite the Allies' misses, it must be said that mankind was fortunate that Hitler decided not to use those weapons. Even after he gave his consent for their deployment, Speer and his other colleagues

---

40   Robert Harris and Jeremy Paxman, *A Higher Form of Killing*, p. 68.
41   Ibid., p. 69.

shot down the proposal. In fact, several of Hitler's close aides had gone against him towards the end of the Second World War. Speer had actually stopped the supply of raw materials needed for the production of chemical weapons. He opined, 'The use of these hazardous chemicals would not only cause large-scale manslaughter, but at the same time have no bearing on the result of the war.' When Hitler's defeat looked imminent, Speer cleverly chose to become an informant.

On the ground, the Allies too were busy with their own attempts at victory, and Britain was at the forefront. In a country that was the epitome of democracy, an entire island was reserved for chemical weapon research and development. No one was allowed entry there till recently. A red light signalling danger was permanently lit there with a board that read: 'This island is government property under experiment. The ground water is contaminated with anthrax and dangerous. Landing is prohibited.'

This was Gruinard Island,[42] located in its own well-protected bay, close to the fishing village of Aultbea, off the north-west coast of Scotland. The British turned the sylvan island into a graveyard in no time. The first recorded trial happened here in 1942. On a summer evening that year, a troop of renowned British virologists and microbiologists arrived, including leading bacteriologist W.R. Lane; Dr David Henderson, a leading member of the Lister Institute; Donald Woods, head of the bacterial chemistry department of London's Middlesex Hospital; Graham Sutton, in charge of all experimental work at Porton Down; and other members of the Royal Society. It also included Dr Paul Fildes, arguably Britain's top bacteriologist at the time—a Fellow of the Royal Society, founder of the *British Journal of Experimental Pathology* and editor of the great nine-volume System of Bacteriology series published by the Medical Research Council in 1931. The presence of these famous scientists at

---

42   Ibid., pp. 70–76, 83, 86, 96, 98, 102.

Gruinard Island in the summer of 1942 was a closely guarded secret under the orders of Prime Minister Winston Churchill.

The preliminary work for these experiments had already been completed by scientists in their laboratories and only their effectiveness had to be tested. For that, they had to explode a bomb containing the substance. The samples were brought to the island; Henderson and Major Allan Younger carefully filled it into the bomb, making sure that not a drop spilt. It was a 25-pound chemical bomb, 18 inches high and 6 inches in diameter.

Its first victims were sheep. Porton's agents had scoured the local hillsides, paying shepherds good prices for their highland sheep. The shepherds had no clue why there was such a steep demand for their sheep all of a sudden. Around thirty animals were collected and left to graze in a field close to the scientists' base camp. As the date for the experiment approached, they were herded into a landing craft and ferried across the half-mile stretch of water to Gruinard. After the bomb had been filled, it too was ferried across, along with Sutton, Henderson and Younger. The anthrax weapon was placed on a small mound of earth. Around it, tethered in concentric circles, were the sheep. An explosive charge was carefully attached to the bomb and a fuse laid. While the sheep grazed unconcernedly, the scientists retreated to a safe distance downwind. When it exploded, billions of spores formed an invisible cloud, which drifted over the terrified sheep and gradually dispersed over the testing site and the sea. At the end of the test, the scientists made their way to a nearby beach where each one of them was stripped to his underpants by an army sergeant who burnt the contaminated suits. Then the scientists were given a thorough shower. Even the ashes of the burnt clothes were destroyed. The men were then rowed back to the camp.

The results of the test began showing the very next day. The sheep began to die, and the pile of carcasses grew larger by the day. The scientists were mighty pleased and hugged each other in glee and informed the Prime Minister about their success. He, on his part, sent a letter of appreciation to the scientists.

The success of the first anthrax bomb in the world was celebrated by everyone. We look at world history through our 150-year-old, thick lenses. We look for heroes and villains. And we applaud everything that the hero does and condemn every act of villains. We refuse to accept that the hero could also have villainous streaks while the villain too could be good in certain aspects. That is why many would find it difficult to digest that Churchill had given his go ahead for the use of these biological bombs. England kept its efforts in developing these inhuman bombs and Churchill's role in this regard a secret for a long time. The British Ministry of War released the papers related to these events only in the 1990s. On the basis of these papers, some historians gave chilling proof of England's role and helped in breaking our long-standing perceptions.

Towards the end of 1944, Churchill expressed his views about the use of biological weapons openly in a letter to the then chief of the army.[43]

I want you to think very seriously over this question of poison gas. It is absurd to consider morality on this topic when everybody used it in the last war without a word of complaint from the moralists or the Church. In the last war the bombing of open cities was regarded as forbidden. On the other hand, everybody does it as a matter of course now. It is simply a question of fashion, changing as she does between long and short skirts for women.

He continues unequivocally in the letter:

I want a cold-blooded calculation made as to how it would pay us to use poison gas, by which I mean principally mustard.

---

43   Ibid., p. 89.

If the bombardment of London really became a serious nuisance and great rockets with far-reaching and devastating effect fell on many centres of government and Labour, I should be prepared to do anything that would hit the enemy in a murderous place. I may certainly have to ask you to support me in using poison gas. We could drench the cities of the Ruhr and many other cities in a way that most of the population would be requiring constant medical attention. I wouldn't want our good manners to be an impediment to our efforts.

These letters prove that Churchill was ready to resort to drastic means. Some may argue that there was no other way to tackle Hitler and grace had no place, but the real shocker is Churchill's desire for Britain to be loaded and ready to use chemical weapons long before Hitler became prominent on the world stage. Since then, there has been ample proof of Churchill's role.

In 1917, the Ottoman Empire fell and the British set up their base in Iraq. The local Arab and Kurdish people protested strongly against the British, and within three years there was great public discontent. The British didn't know how to defuse the situation. Churchill was then the minister of munitions, and his autocratic style of functioning was obvious. He wrote to his military generals in Iraq on 19 February 1920, inquiring whether chemical weapons could be used against the local rebels:

I don't understand why there is so much hashing over the use of chemical weapons. I am fully in favor of employing chemical weapons against these barbarian groups. I believe that the use of these is a scientific necessity.[44]

This was how firmly Churchill had advocated inhuman chemical weapons, which proves that we do not look at history objectively.

---

44   Ibid., pp. 109–18.

The firmness we so admire in our own leaders is considered shamelessness by our adversaries. US Congressman Henry Gonzalez put forth our common lack of objectivity and favouritism while addressing the House of Representatives on 24 March 1992 on the subject of the US's high-handedness in West Asia. Gonzalez, as reported by the US media, was of the opinion that America must exercise its power in that part of the world. In his rebuttal to those who were criticizing US politics, he said, 'Who will decide what is moral?' The first person to decide that it was deploying so-called inhuman chemical weapons was Winston Churchill. He never found their use immoral.[45]

Even before the fatal wounds inflicted by the First World War had healed, Churchill, a strong proponent of chemical warfare, decided to use newer and more powerful chemicals in the Second World War. This was not surprising at all; even his predecessor, Neville Chamberlain, was more than ready.

The British biological warfare project was born on 12 February 1934 at a meeting of the Chiefs of Staff.[46] After the unanimous acceptance of the project, the committee chose Sir Maurice Hankey to head it. The fifty-seven-year-old had become England's counterpart to General Shiro Ishii of Japan. Just as the Japanese owed their venture into the field of biological warfare to Ishii, Britain owed hers to Hankey. He was respected as one of the most powerful officials in the government, not only secretary to the cabinet but also secretary of the Committee of Imperial Defence. In September 1939, Sir Hankey, now with a seat in the House of Lords, was brought into the war cabinet as a minister without a portfolio—testimony to his influence in England.

The British took into account his ability to take unemotional decisions when it came to the development of biological weapons,

45   Giles Milton, 'Winston Churchill's Shocking Use of Chemical Weapons', *The Guardian*, 1 September 2013.

46   W. Seth Carus, 'A Short History of Biological Warfare', National Defense University Press, August 2017.

appointing him chairman of the newly created Microbiological Warfare Committee in 1936. The same year, Hankey proposed to the Committee of Imperial Defence that 'an expert official body' be set up to 'report upon the practicability of the introduction of bacteriological warfare and to make recommendations as to the counter-measures'. The discussions took place in the presence of Prime Minister Chamberlain himself. There was a lot of seesawing on the actions that needed to be taken based on the report, but in 1939, Hitler's army hit Poland hard and the Chamberlain administration was jolted out of inaction. The Prime Minister's Office ordered a speeding up of the research into germ warfare. In fact, Chamberlain had been told that Britain's experimental program is only for self-defence and to give it greater knowledge to protect against such methods. The work was to be conducted in this spirit and not with a view to resort to such methods. With the green signal from the Prime Minister's Office, Britain began its research in earnest into offensive biological weapons. Its first step was to establish a new, top secret laboratory at Porton Down in 1940. It already had the infrastructure to manufacture chemical weapons. Well-known scientists got down to work with only one agenda: to make Britain ready for biological warfare at the earliest because the war was in its second year and the possibility of Hitler attacking London was increasing with every passing day.

In this state of fear, the government recommended the compulsory pasteurization of milk and the chlorination of all supplies of drinking water. England was so sure about Hitler's attack with biological weapons that it procured 2,35,000 doses of an antidote to botulinus toxin, the most feared of biological weapons. Hankey and company requested the Prime Minister on 7 December 1941 to change the original proposal where they were working on germ warfare only for self-defence. They now wanted approval for using it even without provocation.

On the same day, across the Atlantic, Japan attacked the US at Pearl Harbor. It is not certain whether it was a mere coincidence, but the timing was perfect. Two weeks later, Churchill flew to the US for the first Washington Conference, leaving the whole subject in the hands of the Chiefs of Staff. On 2 January 1942, the Defence Committee met in Churchill's absence and discussed biological warfare. A resolution was passed for the use of biological weapons and the minutes of the meeting were recorded in typical, discreet government fashion, saying, 'Lord Hankey was authorized to take such measures as he might from time to time deem appropriate to enable us without undue delay to retaliate in the event of resort by the enemy to the offensive use of bacteria.' The next line in the resolution is telling: 'All possible precautions must be taken to avoid publicity on the subject.' This meant that whatever Britain was going to do from then on would be kept secret.

The resolution authorized the production of massive stocks of anthrax organisms. The testing of anthrax bombs was already in progress on Gruinard Island. Initially, Britain's target was to produce 20 lakh anthrax bombs, which was soon revised to 50 lakh. These were not 'bombs' in the real sense and in the way we imagine them, but small objects like biscuits or circular cookies with holes in them, like Polo mints. The hollows were supposed to be filled with anthrax spores and sealed. The British planned to airdrop these from planes over the German countryside.

The project was progressing on a war footing, and half a dozen filling machines were installed, operated by trained workers. Meanwhile, the success of the Gruinard Island anthrax bomb gave a further fillip to the project. Now, the British were confident of spreading the anthrax bacteria among animals as well as human beings. It was not very harmful in its most basic form and only produced large, fluid-filled blisters on the skin. Once it got serious, it led to septicemia. The important aspect was that if it became an outbreak, ulcers could form in the lungs and kill the patient. However, England put the deployment of the anthrax bombs on the backburner; if it hadn't, the calamity would have been really serious. These bombs would have killed thousands of cattle in Germany and the economic crisis after the Second World War would have been far more critical.

Even then, England was not free from the sin of biological warfare. It kept its involvement in biological warfare hidden for a long time. Then came the audacious Operation Anthropoid, under the leadership of Paul Fildes, with the blessings of none other than Winston Spencer Churchill.[47]

The head of the Nazi police or Gestapo, Reinhard Heydrich, was a major thorn in the flesh of the Allies.[48] He had single-handedly shaken the foundations of the Allies in Europe. He was said to be Hitler's personal choice as the man to succeed him as the Führer. Hitler knew it was vital to control the other European nations to manage Germany's post-war economy as they had a large-scale agricultural and industrial production set-up. He had to separate Britain from Europe by all means. To rub salt into British wounds, he went ahead and appointed Heydrich the *reichsprotektor* of Bohemia and Moravia in September 1941. This small region was a major settlement for Czech workers, a part of Czechoslovakia that had Germany on one side, and Poland and Austria on the other. Heydrich made the Czech workers his own by reducing their working hours and increasing their salaries in return for enhanced production. He improved weekly payouts to farmers and ensured that both these classes were happy with him. The British wanted this region to be under turmoil and challenge Heydrich's power. But none of their efforts worked. They had only one option left—to kill him. The British secret service made

---

47   Robert Harris and Jeremy Paxman, *A Higher Form of Killing*, pp. 91–96.

48   Ibid., pp. 203.

an elaborate and daring plan and decided peak winter in December would be the best time to execute it.

On 29 December 1941, a Halifax bomber airplane took off from the Tempsford airfield and reached Czechoslovakian airspace in four hours. It was impossible for it to escape German radars, and so the British dropped bombs at another place to throw them off track. While the German planes flew off in that direction, the British plane entered Bohemia.

In a small village named Lidice, there was a small, snow-covered hillock. As the plane flew over the hill, seven Czech soldiers—trained at the SOE Special Training School in Scotland—parachuted into it. Apart from conventional weapons, they carried special hand grenades about which they themselves had no clue. They were under strict orders to deploy them at a particular time and place.

These 'Anthropoids' were led by Jan Kubis and Josef Gabcik, who had excellent local connections. The moment they landed in Lidice, they dispersed into the crowd in Bohemia and lived as locals for some time. They were underground for almost five to six months, with only one task—to study Heydrich's daily routine to the last detail.

On 23 May 1941, by a stroke of great good fortune, the Anthropoids learned where Heydrich would be in four days' time. On 27 May, he was supposed to return after meeting Hitler and go to his office via a town road close to Prague. Knowing this, the men did a reconnaissance to find the right spot. Just before Prague, the road curved sharply and all vehicles had to slow down there. Heydrich would be no exception!

They sat crouched close to the spot; four of them with their submachine guns and the special hand grenades, and one with a mirror to flash a signal when Heydrich's car rounded the bend. Rela Fafek, Gabcik's girlfriend, was to drive a car ahead of Heydrich. According to the plan, she would wear a hat if he was coming unescorted. It would take Heydrich two minutes to reach the bend. As planned, Heydrich's green open-topped Mercedes came around the corner exactly two minutes after the mirror signal, and Rela drove past wearing her hat. As his car came close to the bend, Rela slowed her driving pace even further.

Gabcik and Kubis had been waiting for that exact moment. Gabcik strode into the middle of the road and aimed his submachine gun at the bend. As the car slowed, Heydrich screamed at his chauffeur to put his foot on the accelerator, but the driver, a last-minute replacement, kept slamming the brakes. Gabcik pressed the trigger of his submachine gun, but it had got jammed and didn't fire! Kubis realized what was happening, and without wasting a moment, lobbed the grenade towards Heydrich's car. It had come to a complete halt and Heydrich was instructing the driver. The bomb hit the car and the door went flying. Heydrich too got thrown out due to the blast, and shattered pieces of metal and shards of glass spread all around. Splinters from the exploding grenade got lodged into Heydrich's body. He leapt onto the road, shouting and screaming. Suddenly, he dropped his revolver, clutched his right hip, staggered backwards and collapsed.

The gunmen escaped.

Heydrich, in considerable pain and bleeding from the back, was driven, fully conscious, in a commandeered van to the nearby Bulovka Hospital. The doctor on duty in the surgery department was Vladimir Snajdr. Heydrich himself narrated to the doctor everything that had happened. Dr Snajdr checked him and administered first aid. On Heydrich's orders, the local German doctor, Prof. Dick, was summoned. He examined the wounds and found that they were quite deep. Heydrich was asked to sit in a wheelchair to be taken for his X-ray, but he refused and walked courageously to the X-ray room. Everyone could see he was in immense pain.

The X-ray showed no damage to his spinal cord, and his kidneys, too, were normal. It revealed a wound a few inches deep in the upper chest, close to the ribs—a splinter from the bomb which could be removed with a simple local surgery using only local anesthesia.

That is exactly what the doctor did. He applied a local anesthetic and tried to remove the splinter with a superficial incision. But it was lodged deeper than he thought. Heydrich's condition warranted surgery because one rib was broken, his thoracic cage was open, a bomb splinter was lodged in the spleen, and the diaphragm was pierced! It turned out that he had to be given general anesthesia. The doctors told Heydrich this, but he insisted that a surgeon trusted by Hitler be brought there from Berlin. He was not prepared to be anesthetized by anyone else and was ready to put up with pain even if it took hours for the doctor to arrive from Berlin. Dr Dick told him that an immediate operation was required but Heydrich refused to budge.

When he finally relented, he agreed that Prof. Hollbaum of the German surgical clinic in Prague be called in. He was taken to the aseptic theatre and successfully operated on. The bomb splinter embedded in Heydrich's chest was removed. The entire hospital was swarming with German security personnel within minutes. No one other than the doctor who had come from Germany and the surgeon who performed the operation was allowed anywhere near Heydrich. Security was so tight that when a Czech doctor tried to go to the floor where Heydrich was admitted, he was moved out like an ordinary spy.

However, on 4 June, Heydrich suddenly collapsed and died. He had suffered facial paralysis and soon slipped into a coma, never regaining consciousness and dying exactly seven days after the attack. Everyone was baffled by the sudden deterioration, because his condition had actually begun to improve after the surgery and he was walking and speaking normally. It was a big shock that left even the best doctors clueless. It was clear that there was more than what met the eye.

Germany's suspicion proved correct. The official reason reported for his death was septicemia, a condition in which several parts of the body get infected and the infection spreads to the blood and also ends up in the lungs at times. The British had attacked him with a germ bomb containing Clostridium botulinum, which causes botulism. It was a two-pronged attack; the first being the machine guns, and the second the germ bombs contained in the hand grenades, to ensure that even if he escaped the guns, he would surely die. Botulism can spread through the food pipe or open wounds—in Heydrich's case it was the latter. These organisms start showing their effect within two days of infection, and affect muscular function. The eyelids and facial muscles stop functioning, paralysis strikes, and in the absence of the right treatment, leads to death.

The doctors could never have guessed what afflicted Heydrich, and obviously couldn't treat him for it. Hitler was extremely peeved on seeing his successor die such a death, and he took out all his ire on the Czech people. Ten thousand Czech citizens had to pay with their lives for the death of a single associate of his. Both Kubis and Gabcik were caught and killed. But even that wasn't enough to calm his rage. According to some historians, the German intelligence agencies could never recover from Heydrich's death. In accordance with Hitler's orders, he was given a royal funeral in Berlin. After giving his eulogy, the Führer placed a wreath on Heydrich's grave, and asked for the words 'Iron-hearted Man' to be engraved on his tombstone.

The British expected a major revolt to follow the persecution of the Czechs by Hitler, but instead it was the British they were up in arms against. They were irate with them for killing Heydrich, but no one knew how they had done it. The details had been kept under wraps, and murmurs and rumours floated around for many years.

After the Second World War, during the Nuremberg trials, when Russia demanded that the officers, scientists and technicians involved in biological warfare be executed, England opposed their demand. It was scared that if something like that happened, its own role would be revealed. The US and British deceit after the war was such that both nations had their eyes on the German scientists, but it was the Americans who took the lead.

Post-war-weakened Britain had lost its superpower status to the US. Soviet Russia was to become America's prominent competitor. Considering all this, the US offered asylum to all the war-tainted German scientists. US President Harry Truman put together a secret plan called 'Operation Paperclip'. Under the plan, not one, not two, not a hundred, but 760 German scientists who had committed indescribable atrocities on the Jews under Hitler were given asylum in the US. Shiro Ishii of Japan, Major General Walter Schreiber, Kurt Blome, Herman Baker and several other scientists lived peacefully in the US thereafter. A lot of them were involved in biological weapon development and research. The heinous acts that these scientists were doing for Hitler until then were now being done for democracies like the US.

Even so, till as recently as 1980, England claimed never to have manufactured any biological weapons. When a committee to survey chemical weapons manufacturing was set up the same year, the British representative swore the same. But many historians later found evidence of how hollow the claim was. While Germany was disgraced and vilified for the sin of biological warfare, the victorious Allies almost went scot-free. Even if it was true that the victory of the Allies and the defeat of the Germans was a necessity of the time, it has to be accepted that the hands of the victorious were stained with the blood of innocents in equal measure.

Another nation that was neck-deep in such bloodshed was Soviet Russia. Its role in the Second World War remained under wraps and it took several years for the spell of Russia's red philosophy to be broken.

7

From Russia, with Love

NOT much cognizance was taken when a particular bit of news first came out, and nobody remembers the date either. It was certainly in the month of October 1979. The tabloid newspaper in which it first appeared, *Bild Zeitung*, was not very well-known anyway, its main readers being French refugees living in Frankfurt. The news hardly made a stir. The tabloid published the news yet again within three months, in January 1980. This time it got noticed.

'A major accident occurred at the Soviet military research facility in Sverdlovsk in which around thousand people died.'

A few German newspapers picked up the news, and the English newspapers in Frankfurt informed their head offices that some accident had occurred in Russia. Newspaper headlines had said that 'the Russian military had taken control of the area and cordoned it off and no civilians were allowed anywhere near it'. Everyone soon realized the seriousness of the situation. The moment it appears that something is being kept under wraps, it generates that much more curiosity. The Western media tried every trick to get more information—it had been a month since the Russian army entered Afghanistan, and that country was going to become the flashpoint for the Cold War between Russia and the US. This news was very important given that context. For such a significant event, its seriousness has not been realized even after thirty years.

The military base near the city of Sverdlovsk[49] wasn't just another facility of its kind. Biological anthrax bombs were being manufactured here, containing germs of a type that affected the lungs. The bombs could be dropped from the air and were being worked on in this facility. The spores needed to be dried in an apparatus with a filter that had to be cleaned or replaced frequently. One night, a worker shut the machine that filled the spores into bombs and removed the filter but forgot to fix it back. He wrote a notice that said, 'The filter has been removed. Please do not start the machine.' The workers in the night shift didn't see the notice and switched the machine on.

The anthrax spores got thrown out into the air through the chimneys. Waves of the late-night breeze carried the spores into the village nearby. The germ cloud travelled for almost an hour. The moment the workers realized what had happened, they scurried around and shut down the unit, but the damage had been done. The germ spores were about to cause many deaths!

The effect of the anthrax spores that escaped from the unit on 2 April 1979 was seen for another ten days—105 to 1,000 people fell victim, but the exact number is not known till today. Nobody even bothered to count the number of animals and birds that perished.

The hospital records and the autopsy reports of the dead were destroyed because Soviet Russia wanted to keep the entire incident

---

49   Ken Alibek, *Biohazard: The Chilling True Story of the Largest Covert Biological Weapons Program in the World–Told from Inside by the Man Who Ran It*, pp. 70–76, 106, 131; Jeanne Guillemin, *Biological Weapons*, pp. 17, 141–43, 166; Robert Harris and Jeremy Paxman, *A Higher Form of Killing*, pp. 223, 224, 246.

secret. Till date, it has refused to accept that something like this ever happened. Though it had to do so later, Russia still hasn't revealed the exact number of people who lost their lives in the unfortunate accident in Sverdlovsk. It was reported that the dead bodies were dipped in disinfectant liquids and tied up in plastic bags filled with medicines before being taken for burial. This was done to prevent the anthrax spores from leaching into the soil.

A piece of information surfaced years later that said that this biological bomb-manufacturing facility was erected based on know-how received from Japan. Russia, as reported, had focused its attention on the biological weapons research centre in Manchuria during the Second World War and found important research documents from Japanese Unit 731. Even the Americans wanted to get them but the Russians beat them to it. Then they set up the centre at Sverdlovsk. Today, it is known as Yekaterinburg, and the incident is remembered as the Chernobyl of biological warfare. This place, 1,450 km from Moscow, still exists, secured by an army of guards and black Rottweiler dogs. There is a veil of secrecy even today. Back then, as soon as news of the accident came out, local communist district officials rushed there to provide help but the military guards refused to allow them in. Even the highest officials of the ruling government were denied access. They were angry but could do nothing.

In fact, Russia had no intentions of even admitting that the accident had taken place. Following a public outcry it released a statement which said, 'It is true that there has been an anthrax outbreak in these premises, but it was caused by some of the villagers consuming stale beef.' It bandied about the same story for several years. Around the same time, US President Ronald Reagan accused the Soviet Union of producing biological weapons and breaking the international treaty, but this allegation was refuted equally vociferously. Around nine years passed with this status quo.

The wheels of history took a massive turn, steered by Soviet leader Mikhail Gorbachev's vision of *glasnost* and *perestroika*. Under these plans, Gorbachev decided to unilaterally withdraw Soviet troops from Afghanistan, and the Cold War fizzled out. It was Gorbachev who gave orders to exhume the graves of the 1979 anthrax incident victims. Not a word had been printed in the Soviet media about the incident till then. The picture changed with the arrival of Gorbachev and suddenly there were articles on why it was important to investigate the incident. Despite all the hue and cry, Russia did not take responsibility. British Prime Minister Margaret Thatcher played a pivotal role in ensuring that the truth came out eventually. She was on an official visit to the Soviet Union in 1990, the first such visit to the region by a prominent world leader following the Soviet military withdrawal from Afghanistan and the waning of the Cold War. The visit garnered a lot of attention from the world's media. It supposedly went as per plan, with visuals released of Gorbachev and Thatcher shaking hands and smiling cordially in front of mediapersons. But the reality was totally different.

Margaret Thatcher had exposed Gorbachev and the Soviet Union's duplicity with all the hard evidence she had come prepared with. A few months before this meeting, the British secret service hit a major windfall. Vladimir Pasechnik, a reputed Russian biologist and bioweapons engineer, defected to the United Kingdom. He revealed details about the chemical and biological weapon research and development programme in Russia. Armed with this information, Thatcher met Gorbachev in the Kremlin. She had planned to shut him up with the evidence, but didn't succeed because the acceptance of the accident that the Western countries were seeking from Gorbachev never came.

However, things changed drastically within the next two years as the Soviet Union began to break up. Boris Yeltsin, who succeeded Gorbachev, wrote the final chapter of the disintegration of Russia.

On his trip to the US in February 1992, he admitted in front of President George Bush Sr, 'An accident had occurred in Sverdlovsk and we have been duping the world till now.' He did not stop with this confidential admission, going on to announce publicly on 27 May: 'Yes, the Soviet Union had broken the international treaty and was manufacturing biological weapons. Russia's admission was reported extensively by international media. What happened in Sverdlovsk in April 1979 was because of the accident in the biological weapons manufacturing facility.'

He was asked, 'If you were aware of the truth all along, why didn't you speak until now?' He responded, 'The KGB gagged me. I was the communist leader who had gone to Sverdlovsk the night the accident took place. I was stopped from going to the accident site. My voice has been suppressed ever since.' Yeltsin was apparently so peeved at being prevented from visiting the accident site that he even tried to jump over the walls of the military base. His pent-up rage from then came out years later in the form of public acceptance of the sins committed by his country. Many Russians must have found it difficult to digest the culture shock inflicted by Yeltsin's confession because until then there was no power that could make the Russian government seek pardon.

In fact, Russia was an old hand in the game of biological weapons manufacturing compared to other powerful countries like England. It had planned and begun executing its search and manufacture of new, fatal biological weapons even before the end of the First World War. The Bolshevik government was in danger in 1917 with the anti-communist powers posing a major challenge. Around 1 crore people died in the four-year-long conflict between the leftists and the rightists. A vast majority of deaths was caused by a famine and a fatal epidemic,[50] which wasn't an ordinary outbreak by any

---

50   Jeanne Guillemin, *Biological Weapons*, pp. 57–60.

means. Nobody realized what was happening initially because the disease was such. It was called 'typhus', but was totally different from typhoid, which is caused by salmonella bacteria. Typhus is spread by infected body lice transmitted from one person to another, not through droplets or air like cold or flu.

Once it infects a person's body, the typhus bacteria enters the bloodstream through open wounds and scratching. The cell membranes are incapable of stopping them. The first signs and symptoms of the disease appear between the seventh and tenth days of infection. The patient develops a hammering headache, with fever. Rashes develop all over the body, and the fingertips and toes go numb. If neglected, they could develop gangrene because of the hampered blood flow. Forty per cent of typhus patients die. This disease had been eradicated completely from several European countries, but it resurfaced following the internal strife in Russia.

The reason for this was that efforts to produce the typhus germ commercially were ongoing at the Russian government level. A separate department to look after biological weaponry was set up at the Leningrad Military Academy in Moscow that was controlled by a government security agency called GPU, which was nothing but a predecessor of the KGB. At the academy, massive stocks of typhus organisms were produced and stored. Chickens were injected with them, and the pathogens were extracted from the blood of infected birds.

Russia was suffering a severe famine at that time, and citizens were struggling to get two square meals a day, but the Leningrad centre was procuring thousands of eggs for production of the typhus germ. The eggs were injected with the germs, which meant the chicks that hatched would be born infected.

Following its success with typhus, the centre was given the responsibility of producing other biological weapons. Branches were opened on tiny islands in the northern hemisphere, and on one of these stood Stalin's secret torture camp in which prisoners from Russian jails were used as labour to erect. Some of them were also used as guinea pigs. There was not much of a human settlement on the island, and work could progress without any public scrutiny. Any mishaps that occurred went unnoticed and unreported. People working on such experiments were sent there in small batches, carrying all the items needed for experiments, along with provisions for five to six months. The men were prohibited from informing even their families about where they were going and what they were doing. Even the animals used for testing were brought there in large numbers.

At one time, 500 monkeys were ordered to be imported from Africa. But the Russian scientists felt that importing so many monkeys from the same source could garner unnecessary attention, and hence decided to source them from different places. Certain specific disease-causing germs were injected into the monkeys and grown in their bodies.

Several Western countries, especially the US, had prepared a vaccine for tularemia. Russia was working at beating the vaccine and spreading the disease. That is why the monkeys were inoculated with the tularemia vaccine before they reached the designated place on the island, ready to fight it. Tularemia is predominantly an animal disease. It was common in the Rocky Mountains in California and in some parts of Europe. It was transmitted to humans through ticks, rats, bats, pigeons, and even cats and dogs. The important aspect of this disease was that it needed an animal to spread it; it couldn't be directly transmitted from one human to another. Once a person got infected, symptoms like chills, fever, vomiting and severe headaches would appear within a week. The person would become incapacitated, weak and bedridden. If left untreated, death was a certainty.

That was why Russia wanted to beat the vaccine by developing strains of the germ that could survive it. It was aware that if the weapon could be used in war, it could render entire enemy battalions useless. Russia had, in a way, admitted a platoon of these germs into its army.

An unexpected event took place while work on the tularemia germ was in progress. In the year 1941, supplies for similar experiments, equipment and chemicals were being transported by rail. As one such train neared Gorky, the area was suddenly bombed by German airplanes. The Russian soldiers on the train panicked and decided to make the train go faster. But they were hindered because it had to halt at the Kirov station, to the west of the Ural Mountains. By mistake, some chemicals and fluids from the train leaked at the station and as a result, the people of Kirov suffered an epidemic called 'Q fever' for quite some time. This disease was unheard of in Russia till then!

Q fever is caused by the bacterium Coxiella burnetii, which spreads through the air. Once the organism enters the body, it takes anywhere from nine to forty days for symptoms to appear. It begins like an ordinary fever but soon gets more complicated, causing terrible headaches and muscular pain, along with diarrhoea. If not treated on time, it may lead to pneumonia. But it is not a fatal disease. It makes patients stay confined for two to four weeks. Owing to all these characteristics, it was the perfect candidate to be used as a biological weapon in war.

Russia conducted several such experiments during the Second World War, and biological weapons were the principal reason why Hitler's victory march was stopped there. These weapons had made the German army sweat in the crippling winters during the battle in Stalingrad.[51] However, Russia denied the use of any chemicals

---

51   Mark Weber, 'Secrets of the Soviet Disease Warfare Program', *The Journal of Historical Review*, Vol. 18, 1999.

against German forces. When the German army was moving from western Russia to capture Stalingrad, it was the invisible tularemia germ bomb that Russia unleashed.[52] The attack was so powerful that thousands of German soldiers died without any treatment. But Hitler had to halt this approach for some time as lakhs of Russian citizens too got infected.

As a result of the war, farming activity in the area was disturbed. The ready, standing crops wilted and rats and bandicoots had a field day. Their numbers increased, causing tularemia to spread faster. The Volga River valley nearby became the epicentre of the epidemic, causing such severe disease that Russia had to send afflicted soldiers in that area on leave. The germ did not distinguish between nationalities. After taking lakhs of Russian lives, the epidemic came slightly under control. The role that the tularemia germ played in stopping Hitler in his tracks at Stalingrad remained hidden in the pages of history and did not get the attention it deserved. All credit went to brave Russian soldiers instead!

After the Second World War ended in 1945, Russia began looking at germ warfare from a more commercial perspective. In their attempts to subjugate Japan, the Russians got their hands on a gold mine of information regarding the Japanese chemical and biological weapons programme the same year. They captured Unit 731, the research facility in Manchuria, and other laboratories run by Shiro Ishii. Documents were sent to Moscow and Russian scientists studied them in detail, estimating the cost and preparations needed to build manufacturing capacities at a larger scale than what the Japanese had. The wheels were set in motion, and Russian research efforts gained speed.

---

52   Ken Alibek, *Biohazard* p. 30.

Joseph Stalin, leader of the Soviet Union, handed the responsibility of this secret mission to his trusted aide, Lavrentiy Beria,[53] head of the KGB. He had a reputation for being extremely perverted and cruel. Within a year of his taking over, the new military base for manufacturing biological weapons was set up at Sverdlovsk, modelled on Shiro Ishii's centre in Manchuria. A few years passed before work began there formally. But Stalin died in 1953 and Beria was sentenced to death and executed on 23 December the same year.

Nikita Khrushchev, who came to power, handed over the facility to the 15th unit of the Red Army. The chief of the Russian military medical corps, General Yefim Smirnov, was given charge of research. Despite being a doctor, Smirnov was totally in favour of biological weapons. He was of the firm belief that such weapons would play a major role in forthcoming wars. He unscrupulously focused his attention on the research and development of these weapons. The programme got such an impetus during his leadership that then Russian Defence Minister Georgy Zhukov made an open statement: In case of a war in the near future, we will use every weapon of mass destruction, including chemical and biological weapons, in full force and that it is readying with massive manufacturing capabilities.[54] The statement was obviously targeted at Washington, and it received the reaction it deserved.

A single instance is enough to prove Khrushchev's support of Russia's biological weapons programme. On 16 May 1963, he ordered Col. Oleg Penkovsky to be arrested and executed.[55] At least two eyewitnesses claimed that Penkovsky was burnt alive. One of them was Vladimir Rezun, Penkovsky's colleague in the Secret Services

53 Thaddeus Wittlin, *Commissar: The Life and Death of Lavrenty Pavlovich Beria.*

54 Jeanne Guillemin, *Biological Weapons*, p.107.

55 Ibid., pp. 134–45.

who wrote in his autobiography, *Aquarium*, about how Penkovsky was shoved into a furnace and made to suffer a gruesome death. Later, Ernest Volkman wrote about Penkovsky being burnt alive in his book, *Spies: The Secret Agents Who Changed the Course of History*.

Penkovsky was accused of treason. The Russian government suspected him of revealing Russia's military secrets to his British and American friends, and selling them almost 5,000 photos of Russia's military bases. Some of them were biological weapons manufacturing units. In fact, Oleg Penkovsky was the son of a military officer who died fighting in the White Army during the Russian Civil War. Oleg was as hard-working as his father and loved his country. But his perception about his country changed post-1960.

Krushchev had brought in drastic changes in his military policies in 1960, but not much had been reported about them till then. Penkovsky, who was in the army, was certain that Russia would deploy biological weapons in forthcoming wars. His opinion was that Krushchev was making a big mistake. Penkovsky was given the responsibility to watch over the British industrialist Greville Wynne, who was actually a British spy. They met at the National Hotel in Moscow, where Penkovsky showed his readiness to reveal his country's military secrets. Britain jumped at the offer and recruited him into their service. He began working as a double agent. While officially being a Russian spy, he was working against his own nation.

While he was in London in April 1961, Wynne introduced him to two other men who were US spies. During the meeting, Penkovsky agreed to work for the Americans as well, and for the next fifteen months, provided Russian information to both Britain and the US. He told his American and British contacts that the Russian military had developed in a laboratory near Moscow a weapon that was colourless, odourless and more dangerous than any other biological or chemical weapon developed till date. When they asked him the name of the project, he just said, 'America'.

That was what Krushchev had code-named his secret biological and chemical weapons development programme. Was it even surprising that he was given a death sentence, considering the importance of the information he had passed to the Americans and the British! Krushchev wasted no time in sentencing Penkovsky to death the moment he was caught. He was shot dead immediately. The impact of his revelations was felt only later. The CIA compiled and released a bogus document called the 'Penkovsky Papers' and used it very effectively to tarnish Russia's reputation during the Cold War.

Of course, this was not going to have any effect on Russia's march towards manufacturing such weapons. Under Operation Enzymes, spearheaded by renowned Russian agronomist Trofim Lysenko, the Russians planned to develop biological and chemical weapons that could affect both plants and animals. Lysenko was well-known for different reasons. He claimed that all genetic theories developed till that time were utter nonsense and tried to prove them wrong in every possible way. He cultivated plants that grew in ice-cold weather in deserts and also grew summer plants in rainy climates. He was so convinced about his work that he believed that even genetically inherited characteristics could be changed. This meant that a person of European descent could be born with the physical features of an African. He had only one word to describe the genetic scientists of the time: bourgeois! Because of his Marxist disposition towards science, he was a favourite of the Russian ruling class. Krushchev's predecessor, Stalin, had given him a strategic position in the government science department. All his dissenters had been silenced and several biologists were rotting in prison. But the sun wasn't going to change direction just because Lysenko said so!

Biologists and genetic engineers were conducting novel experiments in the US, and Russian scientists were getting information about them, but they kept their mouths shut, fearing Lysenko. But the vice president of the Soviet Science Academy,

Yuri Ovchinnikov, realized that if the Russians continued to agree with whatever Lysenko was saying, his country would fall behind the West. He raised his voice against Lysenko and later received support from the future President, Leonid Brezhnev.

Brezhnev was a metallurgical engineer who is believed to have been impressed with Ovchinnikov. His firm belief that 'if we have to develop biological weapons, we need to be aware of the progress that is taking place in the US and other Western nations' convinced Brezhnev that it would be foolish to jeopardize Russia's defence strategy owing to irrational prejudices and biases.[56] Ovchinnikov was soon appointed chief of the newly constituted genetic engineering department, and the world's largest biotechnology and genetic science laboratory came into being during his time in 1973. It was called 'Biological Substance Preparation' or 'Biopreparat'. It was only a year earlier that Russia had signed the international treaty prohibiting the use of biological weapons. But even before the ink had dried, it was pushing forward with just that.

Biopreparat took on an important mission soon after its inception: to produce massive stocks of tularemia, plague, anthrax and glanders bombs. Its headquarters were very close to the Kremlin, but the research facilities were at three secret locations at Sverdlovsk, Kirov and Zagorsk. In the following years, Biopreparat expanded so much that there were a staggering 60,000 people working on forty-seven different projects. The Russians had categorized their biological weapons research and production programme into three divisions. The first was involved with the development of powerful carriers for the biological bombs, and not much secrecy was maintained for it. The second and third divisions were extremely sensitive ones and no one other than the employees were allowed anywhere near the premises.

---

56   Jeanne Guillemin, *Biological Weapons*, p. 136.

Employees of the third division were allowed inside only when they were in special uniforms which consisted of a rubbery, transparent headpiece with a helmet, a body suit, knee-length boots and long gloves. Three different explanations had been prepared for the activities of these centres. One was absolutely false and meant for the common public; the second was also false and meant to spread confusion; and the third was the truth reserved for a select few. For example, the facility at Omutninsk, as far as the public was concerned, was nothing more than an organic fertilizer manufacturing unit, but very few people were aware that it was growing tularemia, plague, anthrax and glanders microorganisms and converting them into biological weapons to be used in war.

The reins of all these activities were in the hands of Kanatzhan Alibekov, a staunch leftist, known popularly as Ken Alibek. He strongly believed that his motherland should possess such weapons in its armoury. 'A strong advocate of chemicals and biological weapons, Ken, initially, showed hardly any respect for human life. The agency he worked for never believed that human life and existence had ever been important ... We never counted human beings in ones, twos or threes ... we count them in millions ... and when you do that, human deaths are nothing but statistics ... but when one odd person dies, it's an accident. When people die in such large numbers, only the numbers matter ...' That was his covert philosophy regarding the manufacture of biological weapons.[57]

Despite having such a massive biological weapons programme, Russia claimed to be innocent. The US didn't trust Russia one bit and used every trick in the book to find out what was happening there. The problem was that the US wasn't innocent either. Its own strategy about the extent and depth to which it should go was dependent on what Russia was doing, for which it was critical to get information

---

57   Ken Alibek, *Biohazard*.

about Russia's programme. Seeing the obstacles in its way, the US decided that the two countries should share information. It invited a large number of Soviet scientists to the country in the hope that Russia would return the favour. It was only one-way traffic initially. Many Russian scientists travelled to the US under the leadership of Ken Alibek. Meanwhile, George Bush Sr put a lot of pressure on Russia for allowing its biological weapons manufacturing facilities to be examined by international observers.

Due to Soviet bio-weaponeer Vladimir Paseshnik's defection and Boris Yeltsin's public acceptance, Russia had to gradually open its doors. Paseshnik revealed to the British and the Americans that 'Russia's biological weapons development programme is bigger than the west could imagine. The weapons USSR had in their possession were at least ten times stronger, more lethal and penetrative than anything the West has seen so far. Coupled with these, USSR also has developed intercontinental rockets that can be used to drop these biological bombs. Entire North America is in its range and the Russians can attack any city they want.'

Following his revelations, Britain and the US began to put even more pressure on Russia. The CIA had been on the lookout for Alibek because of his frequent visits to the US. After his meetings with the organization, Alibek felt that the US government was far more welfare-oriented compared to Russia. One of his observations regarding this is telling: 'Though America was manufacturing biological weapons at the same level as Russia, its focus was always on developing germ-weapons that were curable or those for which vaccines could be developed and the disease controlled. Whereas Russia is intent on developing biological weapons of diseases that had neither cures nor vaccines ...'[58]

---

58   Ibid.

While Alibek was in the US for a final meeting, the Soviet Union was disintegrating and breaking up into smaller countries. The multitude of biological weapons research and manufacturing facilities were spread all over the vast country, most of them under Alibek, but he brushed off the responsibility calmly. In 1992, he moved to the US with his wife and children, determined never to return.

Alibek's defection was a major blow to Russia as a big chunk of information related to their biological weapons programme was now under US possession. He duly spilled the beans. According to him, Russia possessed a staggering 28,000 chemical and biological bombs. The US and Britain were stunned out of their wits hearing the news. Alibek gave a complete comparative presentation about the American and Russian biological weapons programme. One aspect of it caught everyone's attention. While the US was focused on producing biological weapons of diseases that had some cure or vaccines for prevention, Russia's programme actually began where US efforts ended. Alibek proved with evidence that Russia was producing germ weapons that had no cure or vaccines. In 1999, Alibek wrote a book describing his experiences with biological weapons, *Biohazard: The Chilling True Story of the Largest Covert Biological Program in the World* (Delta Books). The book was published in twenty-one countries and the world at large got to know about Russia's deeds. Alibek also gave statements against Russia under oath to the US Congress, almost receiving a sainthood because of his revelations. George Mason University appointed him a distinguished professor in the medical microbiology and immunology department. He was also given the post of director of education in the university and he gained a lot of popularity during his tenure.

Thanks to his association, the university was able to garner a $40 million research grant from the government. Alibek taught students from across the world the concepts of microbiology. He also gave interviews to popular newspapers and magazines that helped him expand his circle and reach a wider audience. US society loves to ride on waves, and it was Alibek who captured their imagination at that time. He too got carried away by his popularity and started dabbling in different things. One of his extraordinary projects was to prepare a mixture of all available vaccines and create a common vaccine that could be effective on any or all infectious diseases. Some people actually believed that something beneficial could come of such a concoction. Alibek claimed that he had succeeded in his attempt as recently as 2003, but faced flak when the reputed medical journal *Lancet* proved him wrong. But Alibek didn't give up. In 2004, he made another grandiose claim, saying that the smallpox vaccine could be used for the treatment of AIDS. He supported his claims with the results of experiments conducted in his laboratory. But he faced a setback even in this attempt and his claims were proved false. Later, he came out with a tonic called 'Dr Ken Alibek's Immune System Formula', supposedly useful for building immunity. But it was soon proved that this formula didn't work. Owing to his repeated scientific failures and his cozy relationship with the pharma industry, he was forced to quit his position at the university on 11 March 2006.[59]

Alibek went on to work full-time at AFG Biosolutions in Maryland where he is the president and chief scientific officer even today. The company is involved in the manufacture of medicines to fight fatal bacteria causing infectious diseases. Alibek later established another company called MaxWell Biocorporation and is its president as well. Despite being headquartered in Washington, the company's main activities take place in Ukraine, where it has made massive investments in medical research. Ukraine was a part of the

---

59   Ibid.; David Willman, 'Selling the Threat of Bioterrorism', *Los Angeles Times*, 1 July 2007.

erstwhile Soviet Union, and several nuclear-weapon-manufacturing centres exist there.

Because of Alibek's business dealings and activities in Ukraine, there was a lot of suspicion about him. Retired US Maj. Gen. Dr Philip K. Russell punctured all his claims. According to him, what Alibek was saying about Russia's biological weapons program and its role in biological warfare was true ... but 'the rest is all bunkum and he possibly has commercial interests in them'. Dr Philip clipped Alibek's wings with his scathing observations.

Thus, history came full circle. The same US whose integrity impressed Alibek so much that he defected from Russia exposed him using the social integrity and openness he so admired! All his claims after defecting proved false without a doubt. But was his praise and appreciation of American fairness and integrity correct?

8

The Intoxication of the Superpowers

A major in the US army, Leon A. Fox was an example of how off the mark one could be.[60] He wrote an article in the March 1933 issue of *Military Surgeon* magazine in which he said: 'Bacterial warfare is one of the recent scareheads that we are being served by the pseudo-scientists who contribute to the flaming pages of the Sunday annexes syndicated over the nation's press. I consider that it is highly questionable if biologic agents are suited for warfare. Certainly at the present time practically insurmountable technical difficulties prevent the use of biologic agents as effective weapons of warfare.'

As a military officer with a medical education, he should have known better. People weren't aware of his ignorance and misplaced confidence. They believed his views and opinions to be true because of his background and the fact that the article had come out in a

---

60   Ed Regis, *The Biology of Doom: The History of America's Secret Germ Warfare Project*, pp. 10–15.

prestigious magazine. In his article, Fox had elaborated in detail the various viruses and bacteria that could cause disease and the improbability of them being used as biological weapons. The tone of his article made it clear that 'the medical field had advanced so much that such deliberate spread of epidemics was nearly impossible. And whosoever says it's possible is just lying'.

The article became extremely popular and its Japanese translation reached Tokyo within two days. An army officer read it and laughed sarcastically, saying, 'These Americans must be mad!' He was certain that what Fox has written was absolutely wrong, even more so because he himself was working to prove that bacteria and viruses could be used as biological weapons on the battlefield in full force.

That army officer was Shiro Ishii, the brain behind Japan's biological weapons programme, and also an army major at that time, like Leon Fox. Ishii would go on to prove what he was capable of very soon. But at the time of Fox's article, he had nothing to fall back on but plain logic. If it was indeed impossible to manufacture such biological weapons, why did the powerful nations of the world come together in Geneva on 17 June 1925 to sign a treaty restricting their manufacture?

Ishii knew the devastation chemical weapons had caused during the First World War. Besides, he had proved that more people had died of diseases like plague, cholera and typhus than in war. He was confident that the US would be forced to change its opinion, if not today, then certainly in the near future. Ishii and his government were so certain of their beliefs that Ishii was given independent facilities to work on the manufacture of biological weapons. At the same time, Germany too had begun work in this regard, testing such weapons at subway stations in London and Paris.

An article was published by Wickham Steed in the British journal *The Nineteenth Century* and *After* in July 1934. He had got his hands on some secret papers that had reports written by officers of the

German army's chemical weapons department. They had detailed accounts of how bacteria could be used to spread diseases along with surveys regarding the same. One of the experiments was really unique, to show that bacteria could travel through air and survive in air, and how the method could be used for sabotage and attack. The teacher chosen to conduct the experiment had to fill his mouth with a solution containing the bacteria and keep it there for some time. He had to then go to his classroom and teach. It was expected that the bacteria would spread in the air while he spoke and affect the students in the class. It proved successful. Thankfully, the bacteria used weren't very harmful and had been chosen only for testing. The purpose of the experiment was to prove that such a spread was possible. It was recorded that if bacteria could be spread so easily in the classroom, why couldn't the same be done over villages by spraying the solution from airplanes or via fans in railway stations?

Steed published all these reports and predicted that 'if the Germans are aware of this technique, then the underground railway system of London and Paris will be their target'. A good reporter can foresee the future, and Steed did that!

Around the same time, an incident occurred in the Paris subway where the ventilation windows in the railway stations were used to spread bacteria, but a major catastrophe had been avoided as the bacteria used weren't very harmful, according to Germany. Steed wrote in his article, 'Such a test has been conducted at the Piccadilly Circus station in London as well.' Nobody refuted nor corroborated the article, but it did spread widespread panic in London. Several MPs expressed their concern in Parliament. Military officers began testing their preparedness on the sly, and many sat with head in hand, wondering what would be the result of an attack like this.

But the giant called the United States of America was deep in slumber. The incident that proved to be the eye-opener occurred in 1939. Dr Ryoichi Naito, a Japanese chemist, arrived at the Rockefeller Medical Research Center in New York on 23 February.

He had no appointments with anyone that day, but he managed to walk into the massive research centre and go straight to the office of the director, Dr Wilbert Sawyer. He was called inside in a few minutes. As soon as he stepped inside, he took out a letter given to him by the Japanese embassy in the US and made an outrageous demand. He wanted virus samples of yellow fever, because Japan too wanted to produce vaccines for it. Dr Sawyer listened to Naito silently and didn't respond. He wasn't convinced about Naito's intentions. In fact, yellow fever was most common in Africa and South America, and Japan was nowhere close to these areas. There was no reason why Japan needed to produce a vaccine for it. Doubt rankled in Dr Sawyer's mind and he did not agree to Naito's demand immediately.

The third day after the meeting, on a Sunday, an employee of Dr Sawyer's office was returning home from the market. A stranger stopped him on the road and asked, 'I need help from you. I will offer you $1,000 if you agree.'

The employee said, 'First tell me what you want me to do.'

The stranger said, 'It's nothing very big. There has been some misunderstanding between one of the officers of my organization and your director … We need yellow fever viruses for research, but your director is not ready to give them to us … If you could quietly get me some in a small bottle, it will be a great help for us and you will get a substantial amount of money.'

The man hesitated, 'Let me ask my senior …'

But the stranger perceived his hesitation as something else. He raised his offer to $3,000, but the employee refused to yield. He maintained his 'let me see' stance and immediately reported the incident to his senior. When the matter reached Dr Sawyer's office, he told the higher-ups and expressed his suspicions about it. But the US government didn't bother to pay heed to his report.

Around the same time, on 4 October 1940, a low-flying plane over some Shanghai villages sprayed some kind of powder on to the ground below. It looked like bird food, and as soon as it landed, flies began buzzing around it, and swarms and swarms of flies began collecting. Once the sun set, rats and bandicoots too got attracted by the smell of the powder.

Within a few days, the entire area was afflicted by yellow fever, followed by plague. Even before the news could spread, the Chekiang province too was affected, and it was only the start. The list of affected areas began growing, and it would be the same story in many places for months to come. The world took notice of the news with concern.

The US finally woke up. Leon Fox's future took a downward spiral and Japan proved that viruses and bacteria could be used to make biological weapons. Meanwhile, the Second World War was in its second year, and a section of the army had realized that sooner or later the US would have to step in. The same section was also afraid that Japan would not rest without bombing a few American cities with these bioweapon bombs. This part of the army had been completely overlooked and neglected. As the news of Japan's atrocities in China came to light, its opinions found takers.

Of course, the US's first reaction was typically bureaucratic. It set up a committee with reputed and important biotechnology professors and scientists from institutions like Johns Hopkins, Yale, Cornell and Rockefeller Institute as members. It was headed by Edwin Fred, a University of Wisconsin biologist, and called the War Bureau of Consultants (WBC).[61] This was only a deception; its real name was the Committee on Biological Warfare but that wasn't an appropriate name so they rearranged the letters. The committee was supposed to study ways of officially using bioweapons. It met for the first time at the National Academy of Sciences on 18 November 1941. The report of Japan's attack on China came out on the ninth

---

61   Jeanne Guillemin, *Biological Weapons*, pp. 57–60.

day from that first meeting. 7 December 1941, exactly ten days later, was going to be decisive.

When Japan attacked Pearl Harbor, the WBC immediately expressed its views, saying, 'America needs to look at the prospect of germ warfare "seriously".' In reality, it means it too now has to manufacture biological weapons. The US gradually increased its scope in this area, so much so that when the war ended, close to 4,000 technologists and scientists were involved in the production of bioweapons in the US.

The background for the US's affairs was based on the activities of its neighbouring nations. Canada was not considered a combative country, but was way ahead of many powerful countries in the production of bioweapons, in prime part owing to Dr Fredrick Banting, a medical professor at the University of Toronto. He had joined the Canadian army's medical corps and served in France during the First World War. He was a very successful scientist and played an important role in the discovery of insulin as a treatment for diabetes. He won the Nobel Prize for physiology or medicine in 1923.

As he watched world political developments sitting in the peaceful environs of Canada, he had the constant feeling that England and France were not as well prepared for war compared to Germany. He was of the firm opinion that the US could never match Germany in newer forms of warfare and tactics. He was alluding to the latter's biological and chemical weapons programme. During a discussion on whether bioweapons were possible or not, Dr Banting had confidently claimed that 'soon technology that could help drop bacteria bombs from an altitude of thirty-five thousand feet would be developed. We need to own such technology before it falls into enemy hands.'[62]

---

62   Ed Regis, *The Biology of Doom*, pp. 22–24.

He didn't stop at making such statements. His focus was on England when he believed that England must develop such weapons as soon as possible—they may not use them but they must be able to respond hundred times more strongly if such weapons are used against them. His argument was that, 'If they have such power, it will prove to be a strong deterrent for the enemy.' He made these statements as part of a detailed representation to the Canadian defence ministry. He presented with scientific evidence that foot and mouth disease, gangrene, several viral diseases, plague, anthrax, botulinum, rabies and more diseases that affected both humans and animals could be spread in enemy territory during war.

The Canadian defence ministry sent his report to their counterparts in England. The self-proclaimed experts in the British government said, 'Even if what Dr Banting says is true, it would be wiser for us to focus on the health conditions of our citizens.' Their opinion was that Britain should find ways of protecting her citizens from bioweapons rather than developing newer ones. Dr Banting found this group ignorant and optimistic, but he couldn't do anything more to convince them at the time. He was sure that the government would have to pay heed to his words sooner rather than later.

That time came within a year. Hitler's Germany invaded Poland and the government was reminded of Dr Banting's words. By that time, Dr Banting had donned his military uniforms and gone to the battlefield, given the rank of a major by the Canadian army. Dr Banting was enthusiastically fighting on two fronts simultaneously: the battlefield and his laboratory. The British took some time to realize the magnitude of the work the maverick was doing, but the Canadian government was fully aware of his capabilities. It had made him the head of two important committees, one related to medical research and the other to aviation medicine. This field is concerned with the maintenance of health and the performance of crew in an aviation and space environment; for example, it studies the impact of high-altitude flying on passengers and crew. Another secret assignment was to study which medicines, chemicals and bioweapons could be sprayed from airplanes. If it was possible, what were the important factors to be taken care of, what were the possible obstacles? These were the areas Dr Banting was working on.

As part of one of these assignments, Dr Banting visited England towards the end of 1939 along with Canadian toxicologist Dr Israel Rabinowitch. They met at the Porton Down laboratory. Dr Banting felt that the laboratory was working on extremely tight budgets and had a lot of constraints. He had solutions for both. He invited England to set up a testing facility for bioweapons on a 1,000 square km barren stretch of land in Alberta, Canada. Dr Banting and Dr Rabinowitch began crisscrossing England and Europe, meeting several biologists and chemists. They told the groups that were indifferent, 'Don't sit idle; Germany has started manufacturing biological weapons on a very large scale.' Their strong argument was, 'In the future, wars will not be restricted to battlefields and soldiers. Even ordinary civilians will be targeted. There is no difference between killing one soldier or ten civilians. By killing civilians or ordinary citizens, it is possible to cause damage to the productivity and economic stability of enemy countries, and that is why citizens will no longer be safe in forthcoming wars.' Dr Banting created an organization with groups that agreed with his views, had a change of mind or were ready for newer experiments. This organization was working on three fronts.

The first was to investigate every possibility related to bioweapons. The second was setting up an expansive programme to manufacture those organisms that could be developed into biological weapons on a commercial level. The third was to keep an eye on developments in other countries. This committee was responsible for going personally and checking any suspicious infection or disease anywhere in the world and finding remedial measures for the same. It was also given the responsibility of spreading awareness. Despite all their efforts, they did not get the kind of response they expected from England. Dr Banting was so annoyed that he taunted the British bureaucrats, calling them 'highly educated asses'.

But an incident was going to occur soon that would make people take notice of Dr Banting's work.

On 10 May 1940, England's premiership went from Neville Chamberlain to Winston Churchill, who kept the defence ministry under his control. The day this transfer of power happened, Hitler's army attacked Netherlands. The very next month, they decimated France. The fear was that whatever biological weapon research France was doing would now fall into Germany's hands. Germany's next target was England. Britain's Royal Air Force was a thing of pride, and the Germans began bombing London in order to pull the Royal Air Force into battle. The tables turned, and those bureaucrats who had opposed Dr Banting and his team took centre stage. As part of this change, the responsibility for England's chemical and biological weapons manufacturing was given to Dr Paul Fildes. The reins of the newly constituted secret division were in Fildes's hands. The fortunes of the lethal laboratories at Porton Down were now certainly on the rise!

A lot of funds and investments were required to keep its future bright. Dr Banting took up that responsibility.[63] He called big names from the Canadian industry and requested them to contribute money for this critical national cause. One such industrialist was John David Eaton, the owner of T. Eaton, the popular departmental store chain. The other was Edward Wentworth Beatty, the owner of the Canadian Pacific Railway Company. Yet another important personality was industrialist Samuel Bronfman. Not many may be aware of his name

---

63   Ibid., pp. 51–53.

today but most people still love his product. Bronfman was the owner of the popular alcohol brand Seagrams. None of them pulled their hands back from contributing towards weapons production and put together $25,000. They also constituted a secret organization called the War Technical and Scientific Development Committee, which employed every biologist in Canada and its vicinity and made them work on weapons manufacturing.

In October 1940, the committee tested its first bioweapon in the Balsam Hill area to the east of Toronto. They first sprayed sawdust from airplanes to see how far it reached, and tested at what height the planes should fly so that they could cover the largest possible area. Once they had all the test results, the scientists mixed the sawdust with typhoid bacteria and sprayed it.

When they were sure their method worked, Dr Banting went to the Canadian government and asked for official permission to manufacture such weapons at a commercial level. Prime Minister McKenzie King was very pleased and gave his assent immediately. The same night, on 19 November 1940, Dr Banting wrote an emotionally charged note in his diary: 'It is certain that thousands of people will die; there is no place for compassion or sympathy ... the only question is whether they will be our people or Hitler's men.'

The news about the Canadian government giving Dr Banting permission for manufacturing bioweapons reached the US before Britain. Vannevar Bush, director of the Carnegie Institution, was the first to hear about it.[64] He was also head of the National Defence Research Committee of the US government, and a consultant to President Franklin Roosevelt. When Roosevelt heard about the significant developments in Canada, his ears perked up. He had to get the details about what Dr Banting was up to at any cost. He put tremendous pressure on the Canadian government and made them

---

64   Ibid., pp. 59–61.

agree to help and provide all that America needed. But as usual, the latter's appetite and ambition were too big. They sought to take direct advantage of Dr Banting's experience and wanted him to provide all his experience and know-how to the US instead of Britain.

But this was not to be. On 21 February 1941, Dr Banting died in a plane crash on English soil. The Canadians were shaken by the timing of the incident. With his death, Canada lost all the progress they had made in the field of bioweapon production. But within three days of the accident, Paul Fildes of England announced the successful testing of anthrax as a bioweapon. He was now going to become an important link between American and British efforts in biological weapons development.

After Dr Banting's death, Paul Fildes came to the fore. Following Japan's attack on Pearl Harbor, the US was shaken out of its slumber and became completely focused on bioweapons. American bureaucrats had been saying, 'We will agree to the Geneva treaty regarding the prohibition of biological weapons.' But now that the preamble had been built, the committee constituted by the American government rewrote its report. Henry Stimson, defence minister in the Roosevelt government, took the lead. He had always been in favour of the US producing biological weapons. In 1932, when the news of Japan attacking Manchuria and its atrocities using biological weapons came out, Stimson did not change his mind.

His policy is popularly known as the Stimson Policy. He was so firm about the US's war-preparedness that his opinions found favour even with Roosevelt's successor, President Harry Truman. Stimson was of the opinion that the US should drop the atomic bomb on Japan. In February 1942, the report on the US's biological weapons arsenal was ready. Stimson studied it and sent it to President Roosevelt with his comments, saying that though 'biological weapons are extremely despicable, America has to conduct these experiments and develop such weapons'.

In fact, the US had begun producing poisonous gases even before jumping into battle. These were being sent to England. The US had set up two gigantic poison gas manufacturing units in Arkansas and Denver for this purpose, and there were 23,000 people working in them. Thousands of 'Lewisite' bombs were dispatched to England from here. Despite this, the contradiction was that President Roosevelt was dead against the use of chemical and biological weapons. He used to say, 'I believe that no country should resort to the inhuman and merciless use of biological weapons on any country, even if they are sworn enemies.' But Stimson and company convinced him to such an extent that close to the Second World War, he agreed that the US should employ these weapons against Germany and Japan.

George Merck played an extremely important role in making this happen.[65] At that time his family owned the small pharmaceutical company Merck, which today is counted among the largest in the world. According to Stimson, it was a frontrunner in the manufacturing of biological weapons. Once Merck got selected as part of the US committee on biological weapons, there began an immediate search for testing sites. The US set up its first biological weapons testing facility in Fort Detrick, an hour's drive from Washington. It was rumoured that prisoners from all over America were brought there as guinea pigs. In line with the US tradition, there was not much hullabaloo about the news and it didn't raise a storm. The testing of biological weapons was conducted without any publicity, and an extremely controversial personality helped keep it that way.[66]

---

65   Ibid., pp. 61–62.

66   Ken Alibek, *Biohazard*, p. 32; Robert Harris and Jeremy Paxman, *A Higher Form of Killing*, p. 98; Jeanne Guillemin, *Biological Weapons*, pp. 61, 71–74; Judith Miller, Stephen Engelberg and William Broad, *Germs: Biological Weapons and America's Secret War*.

The Second World War ended and General MacArthur's army took formal control of Japan. The responsibility of getting Japan back on the rails fell on him and every important decision was taken with his assent. One such important decision was to pardon General Shiro Ishii.[67] In fact, everyone in the US and every country associated with it at that time believed that it would take stringent action against the general. They believed that his fate would be similar to the German Nazi officers. But the US pardoned the man who was responsible for killing thousands of innocent human beings and decided to take advantage of his knowledge, especially for operations at Fort Detrick.

After the war, Russia was constantly demanding that America take action against Shiro Ishii, but the Americans were so shrewd that they used Russia's name to arm-twist Ishii and get all the information out of him. Initially, Ishii refused to open his mouth and claimed that he had nothing to do with Japan's bioweapons programme. General MacArthur himself questioned him, but he didn't relent. When he was given a threat saying he would be handed over to Russia, Ishii finally broke down. But he did have a condition: the US should give him in writing that he and his close aides would be given *laissez passer* and not be handed over to Russia under any circumstances.

Hearing his condition, the American interrogators asked him, 'What will we gain by saving you?' to which he answered, 'Detailed information about biological weapons, not only about their production but information about the experiments that were conducted during the production, along with observations and data ...'

This was exactly what the US wanted, and the deal was made. General Ishii, convinced with all the assurances, presented all his

---

67   Robert Harris and Jeremy Paxman, *A Higher Form of Killing*, pp. 154–56.

information. He explained how Japan had developed biological weapons using anthrax, plague, tuberculosis, smallpox and cholera germs and how these had been tested freely in China. But the Americans were still suspicious. How could they be certain that what he was saying was true? He could get away by cooking up a story to save his life. To check the authenticity of the information, the US decided to visit Japan and see for themselves.

The Pentagon sent two senior biologists from Fort Detrick to Japan. Dr Edwin V. Hill and Dr Joseph Victor arrived in Tokyo on 28 October 1947 and began their investigations. They visited every laboratory and location General Ishii had mentioned and interviewed several people. They collected a lot of information and then reported to the Pentagon, 'Every word of what General Shiro Ishii has said is true. There is no doubt that these people have attained mastery in biological weapon production.'[68]

The Pentagon was shaken because it had been under the impression that General Shiro Ishii was bluffing. If the US had not been able to produce such weapons, how could he have done it? But General Ishii had proved beyond doubt that it was not only the US which could get things right. The Americans realized that had the Japanese used their bioweapons on them out of rage, they would have had no answers. Moreover, the Russians had begun to put pressure on the US to declare General Ishii a war criminal and arrest him.

The Americans were concerned on two fronts: the first was their ignorance and the second that if the general fell into Russia's hands, it would spell disaster. The Pentagon expressed its concern in its report: 'We need to take care of General Shiro Ishii at any cost. The information about his experiments is so detailed and accurate that it will help us save thousands of dollars, and a lot of time as well. We will

---

68   Ibid.

also be able to avoid a lot of life-threatening tests and experiments. We have been able to acquire all this information without any experimentation. Considering our system and our awareness about human rights, we wouldn't have been able to conduct experiments on living human beings. It is America's duty to ensure that we appreciate the importance of this information and see to it that the person and his information do not fall into anyone's hands.'

In short, General Shiro Ishii had to be given full freedom and all his inhuman actions had to be ignored. Along with this, the US started working on gaining expertise in biological weapons production and developing preventive measures for such attacks. This made the military chemical weapons division really happy. The first project these officials took up was to evaluate US preparedness in handling attacks of chemical and biological weapons. For such tasks, the US had set up a Special Operations Division. Its first goal was to check the Pentagon's preparedness against such attacks, and a dummy attack was mounted on the largest office building in the world, the headquarters of the United States armed forces. Men from the newly established Special Operations Division at Fort Detrick simply walked into the massive building and dropped a pint and a half of harmless bacteria into the air-conditioning system. No one had a clue, and within an hour, the bacteria had spread through the entire building, into the offices of top military and defence ministry officers.

It was the US's good fortune that the bacteria were harmless and had not been released by the Japanese. The officers who conducted the attack later reported, 'We are totally unprotected and can be victims of such attacks very easily. Botulinus, cholera, typhoid ... any such disease could easily spread through our country.'

This was the case with one establishment. What about entire cities? The first city to be chosen for a test was San Francisco, and US navy marines released bacteria in an open space there.

Residents were blissfully unaware of what was happening, and those who did feel something chose to ignore it. The results were the same. What the marines had done in San Francisco was easily doable in other cities as well.

The next location for the exercise was the subway rail system. The Special Operations Division men chosen for the task were to travel on subway trains carrying an apparently normal-looking lightbulb which was in fact filled with bacteria. When no one was looking, the lightbulb would be dropped on to the tracks in the middle of a darkened tunnel.

The men executed their plan, got down at the next station and walked away. Nobody asked any questions. The Special Operations Division had made arrangements to measure the results of the experiment. They surveyed ten stations before and after where the bulb was dropped. The results were the same. The bacteria from the bulb had spread easily over the areas and were thriving! Fortunately, they were not the kind. But what if a real germ attack had taken place? The confidence of the US security system was shattered to pieces. It was time for the US to get complete control over biological weapons, by hook or by crook. That was because Russia and the US were forced to face each other in the Korean war in Asia. This was the first skirmish after the Second World War and it brought the Cold War to boiling point.

The Second World War ended with the division of the world into two political sides, the two opposing bullies being the US and Russia. The US feared that Russia was out to paint the world red with its communist ideology while Russia believed that US capitalism and its large companies were converting the world into its market. This is where the world got segmented and the two superpowers tried to force other small countries into their camp.

Take the case of Korea. Soon after the Second World War ended, Russia invaded Korea. A large part of Korea had been under Japanese occupation since 1910 and Russia was now claiming those areas. The US was scared that if Russia wasn't stopped soon, Korea would fall into the hands of the communists. The US sent its troops into Korea from the other side. It was impossible for Korea to hold out between the warring superpowers. The incapacitated Korean army surrendered to the Russians in the north, while the Korean army in the south submitted to the US. That is the reason why North Korea became communist and South Korea came under US control. The two superpowers divided Korea amongst themselves without sparing a thought for Korean citizens. The division was based on the 38 degree latitude that passed between the two parts. The upper half went to Russia while the US pitched its tents in the bottom half. These tents still remain pitched there with their camels inside.

President Truman assigned a task to the National Security Council in the background of the situation in Korea. He wanted them to review the strengths of the US and Russia and evaluate them objectively. A report of the same was prepared, called 'NSC 68'. The report revealed that the US needed to increase its defence budget. It was forced to do so soon enough by the situation in Asia.

Russia tested its atom (1949) successfully, ending US monopoly over the weapon. When the Korean war was about to begin, a revolution was taking place in neighbouring China, with Mao Zedong and the communists coming to power. The nationalists in power under Chiang Kai-shek were overthrown and pushed to the Formosa Islands. The year the Korean war started, Mao's China entered into a pact with Russia. Even if it was just for show, China joined Russia's side. That is why Truman had to face a lot of criticism in his homeland. He was criticized for letting go of a powerful country like China. Many felt that if America had helped Chiang Kai-shek with supplies and aid, he wouldn't have ended up in exile. But this argument was meaningless because China had already been lost. The US tried to heal its wounds with Korean first aid but found its own military preparedness totally wanting.

There was only one way to heal those wounds: biological weapons! America accepted the brutal reality with glee and produced such weapons at breakneck speed. In the process, not only humans and animals, even plants and trees were not spared.

9

Who Burnt These Trees?

IT is not an everyday occurrence for someone to plunge to death from the topmost floor of a five-star hotel. Whenever such an incident happens, it is invariably labelled murder or suicide. Dr Frank Olson died under such circumstances on 28 November 1953, falling to his death from the thirteenth floor of Hotel Pennsylvania. It would have remained just another case of suicide had he not been who he was:[69] a well-known biological weapons specialist who was working on extremely important research at Fort Detrick. He held a lot of influence in the corridors of power and had just been given access to top secret documents, notes and reports. He was dead a few days after he was given that access. It remains a mystery to this day: was it suicide or murder? There were many reasons for this.

The CIA, the US army and the navy, along with the support of some German doctors, were conducting secret experiments where

---

69   Ed Regis, *The Biology of Doom*, pp. 116, 153–54,157–61,178–80, 230–31.

they were attempting to take control of a person's brain and gather information. The German doctors were experts in the area and had a lot of practice working in Nazi concentration camps. They were conducting experiments with a category of chemical compounds called 'psychedelic drugs', some of which caused extreme excitement. The word 'psychedelic' comes from the Greek word 'psyche', meaning 'mind', and 'delin', meaning 'expressed through'. The feelings and emotions that are normally expressed in deep sleep come to the fore under the influence of these drugs. The persons lose their sense of conscience, allowing their mind to be controlled for a brief period of time. The drug lysergic acid diethylamide, commonly known as LSD, produces similar effects.

The secret mind control project aimed at gathering information was called Operation Artichoke. Other psychedelic drugs apart from LSD, like heroin, opium, etc., were used in limited, and in some cases unlimited, doses to study whether a person's mind could be controlled. Research was also done on dosage, time taken for the drugs to kick in, how long it took before the person started following one's commands, and many other such aspects. The CIA was keen to control the working of the human brain with drugs, but they pointed fingers at Russia and China for doing the same. Russia was far ahead in the race. While China too was conducting such experiments, it had not caught up with the US.

It was true that there was a change in the behaviour of the subjects who were given the drugs. Even Dr Frank Olson's demeanour had changed, and he needed psychiatric counselling. His family members claimed that Olson had begun talking about quitting the CIA and become distressed with his work. Some details and aspects of his work that were unknown to him had surfaced and he was shocked and began slipping into a state of depression. The CIA began to keep an eye on him; agents tailed him even when he visited his psychiatrist. Following Olson's sudden death, the CIA declared that he had been depressed and had committed suicide as a result. Everyone seemed to be satisfied with the explanation at that time.

The truth of that statement remained uncontested for almost two decades, but in the late 1970s, the activities of the CIA came under suspicion and scrutiny following the Watergate scandal. One of the issues that drew attention was Dr Olson's apparent suicide. Since a lot of noise was being raised on the issue, the CIA revealed, 'As part of our experiments, we had given Dr Olson LSD for ten days preceding his death and he knew nothing about it. Dr Olson got depressed under the effect of the drug and committed suicide.' The CIA apologized publicly to Dr Olson's family. President Gerald Ford himself met them and sought their forgiveness. The government offered Mrs Olson a hefty compensation as well.

Despite the apologies, Dr Olson's son, Eric, was convinced that the CIA was lying and that his father had, in fact, been murdered. He had been trying to uncover the truth about his father's death for a long time, but his investigations were stuck and not leading anywhere. After the US president apologized, his investigations suddenly picked up pace. Eric Olson got his father's body exhumed and examined by reputed doctors.

The new autopsy report suggested that 'the doctors did find a large hematoma on the left side of Olson's head and a large injury on his chest'. Most of the autopsy team agreed that the blunt-force trauma to the head and injury to the chest had not occurred during the fall, but most likely before it. His body must have been thrown from a height. The report was starkly suggestive of homicide.

The report went public and the Manhattan district attorney filed a case against an unknown killer and reopened the old case. Eric Olson was relieved and felt assured that the accused would now be brought to book and punished. But the investigation slowed down as soon as the investigating agency sent a summons to Dr Olson's colleague in the CIA, Robert Lashbrook. The CIA prohibited Lashbrook from testifying in court. It roped in the White House, and the President's office was sent a letter saying, 'Stop the investigation. We will give them a bigger compensation. Because if the investigation continues, we will have to reveal some very sensitive and confidential information related to national security. If something like this happens, America's reputation at the global stage will be tarnished.'

The letter was dated 11 July 1975, sent by Dick Cheney, and handed over to Donald Rumsfeld, the then Chief of Staff.[70] One more person was involved—George Bush Sr. He too met the Olson family to request them not to stretch the matter too much. His son, George W. Bush, went on to become the President and Dick Cheney the Vice President, while Rumsfeld became Secretary of Defense. All three fought hard to keep the Olson affair secret. A lot of skeletons would tumble out if the truth was revealed.

There were a lot of matters that the US and the CIA didn't want exposed. One of them related to its bioweapons programme. The US could not follow Japan's model in this regard. Its people and media were capable of questioning the legislature and putting pressure on it. Hence, a lot of things had to be done on the sly, bypassing the system. In some cases, serious disease-causing microorganisms were discreetly picked up from government hospitals to conduct experiments on prisoners. These experiments weren't restricted to human beings; even trees were experimented upon to stunt their growth, and studies were done of ways to singe and damage standing crops. US scientists went to the extent of spraying poison on the wings of pigeons and seeing if they could be effective carriers of poison. It was proved that the poison on pigeons' wings could remain dry and intact even if the birds flew 100 km. The background for these experiments was what the US did in the Vietnam war. Though it

---

70   'Cheney & Rumsfeld Linked Murder of CIA Scientist', News at freedomarchives.org, 25 June 2004.

ultimately lost, America's actions at that time are unparalleled in human history.

Vietnam has been an issue for more than a hundred years. The US was paranoid that Russia would play dirty tricks in Vietnam during the Cold War period and got embroiled in the mess to stop Russia, rekindling the fire at a time when the embers of the Korean war had not died down.

The real issue was between France and its centuries-old colony, Vietnam. Matters came to a head when it had to leave the Asian nation in July 1954. After the uprising and internal conflicts there, France realized it could not control things sitting in Paris. Once the decision was made, a meeting for a treaty between both nations took place in Geneva. However, the matter was not to be resolved easily, with both Russia and China getting involved. It was decided to divide the nation into two for the time being, and use the democratic election of 1956 to arrive at a combined entity once again and eliminate the 'imaginary dividing line'.

This stumped the US, which was worried that the communists were getting away with everything. To prevent that from happening, it formed the South-East Asia Treaty Organization (SEATO), similar to NATO. The 'imaginary' line was made real. Two persons played an important role in making this happen: US Secretary of State John Foster Dallas and President Dwight D. Eisenhower himself. The US started making south Vietnam its base and set up a new government there called the Government of the Republic of Vietnam. It got the bitter anti-communist Ngo Dinh Diem on its side and began meddling with Vietnam's internal affairs. As soon as Diem came to power, he began raising slogans against the communists. He felt its government is under threat from the leftists and the Democratic Republic of Vietnam government in North Vietnam is rising against it. In other words, the Diem government wanted the US to save it.

The US poured in so much money, arms and ammunition into Vietnam that the Diem government became arrogant and oppressive. It imprisoned thousands of people on mere suspicion of being communists and made up laws as per whim. According to these, the government could arrest anyone without any charges or investigation and keep them in prison for any duration. They took US support for granted. Initially, the US entered Vietnam as military consultants and mentors, and by the end of 1960, 900 US military officers had pitched tents there. During this time, John F. Kennedy came to power. The biggest crisis for his government was Vietnam. He tried to sail on both boats simultaneously.

But the situation was getting out of control. The communists in Vietnam too had begun getting a lot of support. The communist strategy to bring the two sides together found support from the Vietnamese people as well, and even Buddhist monks joined the cause.

Kennedy had to do something. He decided to send a military unit to Vietnam. Its job was to assess the on-ground situation and decide the role that the US should play there. The unit reported back saying 'send military aid, other supplies and crush the communists'. But a section of the Kennedy administration was preventing the President from taking such a desperate step. In its opinion, 'what has happened has happened'. And that 'America should withdraw from Vietnam'. Kennedy was trapped between two extremes; he finally decided to please both groups by deciding not to send any large-scale military aid, and at the same time not pulling back either. In the meantime, he also decided to sign a pact with the Diem government and send them just enough aid to keep them under control. But the strategy proved wrong from day one.

The communist pressure was so strong that Diem's army began falling apart, and it was evident that the government would soon topple. Diem's brother, Ngo Dinh Nhu, was so annoyed that his special forces raided and vandalized Buddhist pagodas across the country, arresting thousands of monks and causing a death toll estimated to be in the hundreds. He accused the monks of siding with the communists and let the army loose on them. But the result was exactly the opposite of what he had expected. The protesters became more aggressive and the Buddhist monks began immolating themselves. The disturbing pictures were carried by most newspapers around the globe and there was a severe backlash against the US. Diem now became a thorn in America's flesh and made it change its tune, so much so that it became party to a plot to unseat the Diem regime. The US instigated a revolt in Diem's army, and the military coup took place on 1 November 1963. The dissidents arrested the Nhu brothers and assassinated them. John F. Kennedy was assassinated in Dallas exactly twenty-two days later, on 22 November 1963.

There were a lot of things happening in Vietnam that disturbed people like Olson.[71] As the Russian interest in Vietnam grew, the US military presence increased, the head count reaching 11,000 in the first two years. The US then constituted a special military division called the Military Assistant Command of Vietnam, and the number of US soldiers in Vietnam rose to 60,000 over the next two years. The troops became gradually more and more combative, pushing back the North Korean army and dropping bombs in the area. America claimed that 'they had to retaliate' because the Russian army stationed in North Vietnam had become aggressive. Every intrusion or invasion always begins like this. The skirmishes increased so much that in the next four years, US soldiers had pitched their tents in Vietnam. In the entire war period, close to 38 lakh US soldiers were deployed in Vietnam.

71　'Battlefield: Vietnam', PBS, www.pbs.org/battlefieldvietnam/timeline; 'The Virtual Vietnam Archive', Texas Tech University, https://www. vietnam.ttu.edu/virtualarchive/

Despite all this, the Vietnamese conflict was not coming under control. Following Kennedy's death, it proved a huge challenge for his successor, Lyndon Johnson. His tenure as President was stuck between two views, one that felt Vietnam must be defeated at any cost, and the other which wanted American troops to be called back from Vietnam. Withdrawing the troops would be a loss of face, and Johnson rejected that idea instantly. He didn't want the dubious distinction of being the only American President to have lost a war. He took the vengeful and diabolical decision of implementing his predecessor Kennedy's plan, if and when the need arose.

The plan was regarding the use of chemical weapons, but a kind that had never been used before. These weren't harmful for human beings, at least at that time. The target of these chemicals was trees, shrubs and standing crops in fields.[72] Kennedy had given his 'in principle' approval for the use of these chemical weapons in December 1961 under Operation Ranch Hand. These chemical weapons were first tested on 12 December 1961, but Kennedy hadn't dared to use them indiscriminately. In August 1962, he realized that the US soldiers hadn't succeeded in controlling the situation in Vietnam and gave his nod to use the weapons. The very next month, a massive chemical attack was launched on the Ca Mau province in south Vietnam.

The results of the dreadful attack were visible within two weeks. Vietnam is blessed with rich and dense forests. The communist rebels would mount guerilla attacks on US military camps in Vietnam and disappear into the thick jungles where they could not be spotted by US helicopters. If the helicopters flew a little lower to spot them, the rebels would fire and damage the aircraft. That was when US soldiers decided to target the very trees that provided

72   Ibid., pp. 8, 12, 113–17; Robert Harris and Jeremy Paxman, *A Higher Form of Killing*, pp. 170, 172–73, 198, 236.

shelter and cover to Vietnamese soldiers. The chemical weapons were so toxic that soon trees began to shed leaves and were bare within eight days, making it tough for the Vietnamese soldiers to hide. Standing crops used to wilt away in a flash. No one had a clue about what was happening.

President Johnson gave the go-ahead to generously rain toxic chemicals over the forests of Vietnam using giant C-23 planes. Anything and everything that came in contact with the chemical perished. It would be taken to river banks by small boats and sprayed on trees. In some cases, US soldiers would stand in open trucks, spraying jets of it into the air. The entire path they went on would become barren and devoid of vegetation. Towards the end of the war, US soldiers went to every field and destroyed them one by one. Operation Farm Hand had reached its peak post-1967. Thirty-six C-23 planes were readied for the purpose, and there would be three such sorties per day, which soon increased to twelve and then to thirty-nine. The sprayings had been done 1,600 times in one year.

The devastation caused was unimaginable, rendering up to 32 lakh acres of forests barren and destroying 2,47,000 acres of standing crops. Nothing could be grown on the barren land for several years to come, meaning that close to one-seventh of Vietnamese land had gone waste. Almost 48,000 tons of poisonous chemicals had been sprayed on the small country—25 kg per acre, ten times the tolerance limit.

There were mainly four classes of chemicals that were used, identifiable by colour codes on the thousands of cylinders of 55 gallon capacity where they were stored. The chemicals were named based on the colour of the line painted on the cylinder. Agent Orange, Agent Blue, Agent Purple, Agent White and so on. This naming system was devised because the chemical names were complicated; for example, 2,4-dichlorophenoxy acetic acid, 2,4,5-trichlorophenoxyacetic acid, picloram or cacodylic acid.

Of these, the most lethal and frequently used was Agent Orange. It actually entered the fray quite late, much after Agent Blue and Agent Purple. But it became the chemical agent of choice because of its effectiveness.

Between 1962 and 1971, America used 1.9 crore gallons of chemical weapons in Vietnam, of which 1.10 crore gallons was Agent Orange.[73] Like the origin story of many other chemicals, Agent Orange too was developed for a good cause, but ended up being used for harmful purposes.

American biologist Arthur Galston had studied the use of 2,3,5-triiodobenzoic acid for encouraging the flowering of soya bean plants. He wanted to create a breed of soya plants that matured faster. His intention was to reduce the chances of food scarcity. He realized, during his experiments, that if the dose of the chemical became a little excessive, the plant grew too fast and died. He stopped his experiments, but the science didn't stop there.

Ian Sussex, another biologist, continued with Galston's experiments and created a series of herbicides and pesticides to kill weeds and pests, respectively. New chemicals that damaged trees were developed in England and the US. Once these chemicals were sprayed, the plants got trapped. The herbicides worked by acting as duplicate growth hormones, mimicking the natural plant growth hormones to trick plants. They would then grow at a furious rate, completing the life cycle that usually took years in a matter of days. By the time they realized they had been obeying duplicate hormones, their life was over. Gradually, the plants wilted and forests turned into miles and miles of barren land.

These chemicals were collectively used to kill weeds, but were soon sprayed on leaves and roots. Their ill effects were so strong that

---

73   'Chemical Warfare: Use of Herbicides during the Vietnam War',
      https://science.jrank.org/pages/1391/Chemical-Warfare-Use-
      herbicides-during-Vietnam-War.html

Galston took up arms against their use in Vietnam. Like Einstein was worried about the destructive use of atomic energy, Galston too was plagued by similar concerns about his own product.

But wisdom doesn't stand a chance in power and politics, does it? The US went ahead and used these toxic chemicals at will in Vietnam, ravaging the land for nine continuous years. The chemicals seeped in so deeply into Vietnamese soil that their deleterious effects were seen for decades after the war, even to this day. Their effect showed not only on trees and shrubs but also on birds, animals and even human beings dependent on them. The political brutality was such that America was well aware of the lethal effects of these chemicals since 1963 and, subsequently, it constituted a committee to study them. After four years of analysis, the committee noted that the effects of these chemicals were not only lethal, but they are fateful. The victims who came in contact with these chemicals suffer from cancer of the lungs, respiratory passage, blood and other organs. They suffer skin diseases, blindness, sterility, deformed births in large numbers. The committee backed up its claims with hard evidence.

However, these warnings didn't make even an iota of difference and the US continued to use these chemical weapons with extra vigour. The pinnacle of its heartlessness was such that its leaders turned a blind eye to the suffering of not only the Vietnamese but even US soldiers. According to data reported by the committee and the Vietnamese government, close to 4.8 million Vietnamese citizens were reported to have come in contact with Agent Orange. Of them, 4 lakh were fortunate to have died. Many survivors were handicapped and thousands of women who gave birth had children with serious deformities and reduced mental faculties. Some were born with one eye, without a nose or just hollows in place of eyes! An entire generation was born cursed.

Even US soldiers died untimely, gruesome deaths. According to American war records, 58,236 soldiers lost their lives in the Vietnam war;[74] 3,03,644 were maimed for life; and the fate of 1,724 others is a mystery till date. An important point to note is that a large number of US soldiers died during the period when their own country was using chemical weapons on a very large scale. 11,153 in 1967; 16,592 in 1968; 11,616 in 1969 and 6,081 in 1970—these are the statistics that the records show.

This was the magnitude of loss that the US had to bear, but there were far more serious invisible blows. Many who returned home from Vietnam lost their mental balance or suffered stomach cancer, lung cancer and even skin cancer. The number of soldiers who were addicted to drugs was almost uncountable. All these soldiers, collectively called 'veterans', having witnessed so much violence and cruelty, lost interest in life. They were alive, but not living. The US government struggled to rehabilitate them even till the end of the twentieth century.

The US was forced to stop in its tracks around 1969, the same year word came out about the inhuman torture its soldiers had committed in Vietnam. On 16 March 1968, on a single day, the US army killed people en masse in the Mỹ Lai province. Almost 504 people died, all of whom were ordinary citizens, among them 347 women, children and elderly people. The women faced the most barbaric deaths, after being sexually assaulted, gang raped and helpless as their bodies were mutilated.

By the end of the year, the news of the Mỹ Lai massacre spread through the US, and there was widespread public outrage all over the country against the army. First, the revelation of the use of chemical weapons, and then the massacre led to a wave of mass discontent and contempt against the government. As a result, the research wing of the Department of Defense started a campaign to evaluate the

---

74 'Vietnam War U.S. Military Fatal Casualty Statistics', National Archives.

ill effects of Agent Orange. Pregnant mice were exposed to Agent Orange in the lab—it was found that all the newborn mice had some organ or body part missing. The results proved how unsafe and toxic Agent Orange was. The US government passed an order in December 1969: 'Agent Orange will not be used in residential areas.' It was an apt example of shutting the stable door after the horse has bolted.

Furthermore, American callousness was such that they banned the use of Agent Orange with immediate effect but took up Agent White to devastating effect from then on. (It was relatively less grievous compared to Agent Orange.) The details about all these chemical agents came out after the war. Some soldiers and social organizations filed compensation cases against the companies that manufactured them. The court battles began in 1979, with the accused being mega companies which are now familiar to us—Dow Chemicals, Monsanto, Diamond Shemrock, Thompson Chemicals, etc. After eight long years of fighting in court, the accused companies agreed to an out-of-court settlement. In 1987, they agreed to pay a compensation of almost $180 million and the case was closed. The condition was that nobody in any US state would hold these companies responsible for the atrocities in Vietnam. The last case was closed in 1992. The final outcome was that every soldier was offered compensation up to a maximum of $1,200. What a cruel joke!

Although this matter was closed, the mention of Vietnam continue to throw up horrifying names and images, such as napalm bombs and hordes of terrified children moaning and crying in pain, walking on the streets.[75] These children were living testimony to what napalm bombs were capable of. These are not really bombs in the traditional sense. They consist of petrol or gasoline mixed with

---

75   'Munitions', www.globalsecurity.org/military/systems/munitions

other chemicals to keep them burning for a longer time. Gasoline was anyway being used in war to spread fire, but it would get doused very fast and explode all at once. Military researchers felt they needed something that could burn for a longer duration, was dispersed easily and stuck to its target strongly.

The researchers found success during the Second World War. Louis Fieser, a professor at Harvard University, was a well-known name in the field of organic chemistry. He had succeeded in synthesizing the hormone cortisone. While he was working in his laboratory, he thought of dissolving rubber in gasoline. He succeeded, and the volatility of gasoline combined with the stickiness of rubber created a sticky fireball in 1942. This was a deadly combination indeed, if only there wasn't an acute shortage of natural rubber during WWII.

A team of chemists led by Fieser at Harvard University was the first to develop synthetic napalm, a brown, dry powder that was not sticky by itself, but when mixed with gasoline turned into an extremely sticky and inflammable substance. It turned out to be a boon for war and was used for the first time against Germany and Japan during the Second World War. Once its effectiveness was proven, it was included in wartime arsenal. A lot of further experimentation took place to make it more lethal. The final product was the napalm bomb—a combination of the salts of naphthenic acid and palmitic acid. The US used it generously in Vietnam.

Once the bomb was thrown, it would catch fire—but not a regular fire, more like a mix of visible and invisible balls of fire. These balls would then turn into a sort of whirlpool, causing a change in air pressure. Once air entered the whirlpool, it gained speed and moved forward as it burnt. It needed oxygen to remain aflame, and would pull all the atmospheric oxygen towards itself and increase the concentration of toxic carbon monoxide around it. The entire process happened in a flash and the whirlpool attained a speed of 70 kmph.

The temperature would increase to around 2,000 degrees Celsius, like the coal furnace of a railway steam engine. Once it began to move on land, it would burn everything in its path, and anything that survived would die of asphyxiation and lack of oxygen. The air would get filled with carbon monoxide. Even 0.4 per cent of carbon monoxide is enough to kill a human being, while the napalm bomb produces 20 per cent carbon monoxide. The US dropped napalm bombs with 130 gallons of the deadly mixture that produced a fireball 100 feet high, 270 feet long and 75 feet wide. Even if someone tried to hide underground, the heat would reach there. Thus, if a napalm bomb was dropped from above, there was no way one could escape being charred. The heat was such that victims would suffer third-degree burns. The US used these bombs on a large scale to pull out enemy soldiers hiding in trenches. As a result, not only did the frontline soldiers die, even citizens living around the warfront were singed.

The dastardly deed of producing these bombs was done by two companies: Standard Oil, the flagship company belonging to noted US oil baron John D. Rockefeller, and Dow Chemicals, which had earlier produced massive amounts of napalm bombs for the US army from 1965 to 1969. Once the cruelty of these companies became known publicly, there was massive public anger and outrage against them, especially Dow, because Standard Oil's contribution was limited to the production of gasoline. The lethal napalm was manufactured by Dow. It had to take defensive action but only briefly. For the company though moralities in war and human values were important, but it was bound by the safety and security of our US citizen ... 'Therefore, our first priority is the American government,' it noted.

What went unsaid was the massive amounts of money the company received from the government. There was a wave of public discontent in America against all such businesses and a number of protests were organized. Even Canada and Britain were party to these businesses and their roles too were exposed. The heartrending story of Flt Lt William Cockayne, working in England's Porton Down laboratory, came out in the open.

A battery of experiments relating to chemical and biological weapons was being conducted at Porton Down with the support of its close ally, the US, at that time. The Cold War was at its peak, and the two countries had taken it upon themselves to rally against Soviet Russia. These so-called cultured and sophisticated partners faced a very strange problem! Now that Japan, Germany and the common enemy Russia were not part of the heinous project, who would they test their products on? Since Japan, Russia and a few other countries were testing these weapons on human subjects, it was serving America and England's purpose and they didn't have to bloody their hands.

The two powerful nations found an easy alternative: animals. Since the poor four-legged creatures didn't vote, their disfavour or displeasure didn't count! The scientists assembled all kinds of animals at Porton Down: chimpanzees, monkeys, dogs, cows, buffalos, goats, mice and others. The responsibility of keeping an eye on the animals fell on young Flt Lt William Cockayne, a soft-hearted soldier who made the grave mistake of loving the animals. Soon, several of his dear animals were falling prey to chemical weapons and he had to destroy mountains of their carcasses. The numbers increased so much that William was deeply troubled and needed treatment himself.

His story was published in the local newspapers, and it spread like wildfire. Readers' hearts skipped a beat, and there was a swell of public opinion, but the military leadership refused to pay any attention and continued their research on biological weapons with increased vigour. The US literally began producing disease-carrying mosquitos. Their goal was to produce 50 million such mosquitos in a week along with other microorganisms causing mild diseases such as food poisoning, stomach infections and diarrhoea.

When the military officers were asked why they were indulging in such experiments when they already possessed biological weapons, the response of one officer was the epitome of outlandishness. He is reported to have replied, 'When a soldier is suffering severe loose motions, even if he finds his arch enemy in front of him, he won't be able to take aim and hit his target. That is why we need such weapons along with conventional arms!'

The US government faced a lot of public outrage. In the elections following the defeat in Vietnam, Lyndon Johnson gave way to Richard Nixon. He too came under criticism for the use of biological weapons. The Eighteen-Nation Committee on Disarmament meeting was held in Geneva in 1968, where a plan for banning the production of chemical and biological weapons was put forth. In the meantime, several countries had already produced and tested poisonous gases. It was an open secret, but that issue was put on the backburner and Britain suggested that the matter of biological and chemical weapons be discussed separately. Once Britain was certain that the US was on its side, it brought forth a resolution called the Biological Weapons Convention. When Russia realized that the US and England were in collusion, Russia protested strongly.

President Nixon realized that this was a chance for him to prove his supremacy and said somewhat like this: 'Friends, we have ourselves sown the seeds of infertility at a large scale. We must reduce some of those if possible. One of them would be biological weapons. The United States unilaterally renounces the first use of lethal or incapacitating chemical weapons and unconditionally renounces all methods of biological warfare.'[76]

---

76   Reported in Foreign Relations of the United States, 1969-1976, Volume E-2, Documents on Arms Control and Nonproliferation, 1969-1972.

This was on 25 November 1969.

But the damage had already been done. The US did get a lot of support for its declaration and the pressure on Russia too increased and it had to agree. The two countries signed an agreement on 4 April 1972 that they would not use such weapons against each other. They took a public oath: 'We will not manufacture or use these deadly weapons. We will not offer support to any country that manufactures these weapons nor will we procure such weapons from any one.' Once other countries saw that Russia and US made such a public commitment, they too came forward. Close to eighty countries agreed to the terms and conditions of the treaty and decided against the manufacture of biological weapons.

What happened was great but it was too late. The horses had bolted from the stables long ago.

A book was published in the first week of March 2010 in the US. Titled *A Terrible Mistake: The Murder of Frank Olson and the CIA's Secret War Experiments*, it brought to light the circumstances under which Dr Olson died and underscored two important points: one, that many facts remained to be unravelled, and two, that those responsible for the atrocity were being exposed in their own country. Democratic countries like ours have a lot to learn from the second point.

The CIA had created a disaster in the small French town of Pont-Saint in 1951. It took control of some bakeries and contaminated the flour with LSD. The entire population had hallucinations and went crazy. One man imagined he had swallowed a snake and tried to vomit it out. An eleven-year-old boy tried to kill his grandmother thinking she was a witch. Another person imagined his bed was covered with rose blooms. Nobody was able to find the reason behind these strange happenings. It was later found that the intoxicating drug used there was allegedly supplied by the pharmaceutical giant Sandoz. The company was covertly working for the CIA, and

Dr Olson, employed at Fort Detrick, had got to know about it.[77] The reporter H.P. Albarelli researched the dubious circumstances behind Dr Olson's death for over ten years and revealed the truth behind his murder.

---

77   Ed Regis, *The Biology of Doom*, p. 153; Mike Thomson, 'Pont-Saint-Esprit Poisoning: Did the CIA Spread LSD?', 23 August 2010; BBC, 'MK Ultra: The Secrets of the CIA's Mind-Control Programme', 29 March 2022.

10

The Butcher of Baghdad

THE most recent war of our times was fought in 2003. US President George W. Bush had taken up a massive military campaign to unseat Saddam Hussain, the ruler of Iraq. Donald Rumsfeld, Secretary of Defense, had been proclaiming to the world that Saddam Hussein owned large piles of weapons of mass destruction (WMDs), and therefore had to be removed from power. As is normal practice in the US, the press and media were creating a conducive environment for the government. If someone had asked the US to list the top ten dangers faced by humanity at that time, it would have listed Saddam Hussein from one to ten. In its successful creation of an environment and background against Saddam Hussein, England and other nations that leaned on the US gave their support and took part in the campaign. Former England Prime Minister Tony Blair, believing the American narrative, read out a list of Saddam Hussein's atrocities in the British Parliament. This group went about convincing the world about the massive store of biological, chemical and nuclear bombs that Saddam Hussein had accumulated. A few American media houses that survived on government information toed the same line and labelled Saddam Hussein the 'Butcher of Baghdad' and tried to convince us about how important his annihilation was for world safety.

What Rumsfeld and the press were saying was not entirely wrong. The US camel that had entered Iraqi tents found Saddam Hussein, his son and his ministers, but no WMDs. Despite that, Rumsfeld was right.

Twenty years ago, the Americans had tried to get hold of this armoury.[78] In 1982, the then US President Ronald Reagan had shown exceptional generosity and got Iraq's name omitted from the list of terrorist nations. The Congress was against it, but Reagan's love for Saddam Hussein was too strong. The same year, the Reagan administration gave Hussein sixty heavy-duty helicopters, and in December the following year, Reagan sent his special envoy to Baghdad to offer support to Saddam Hussein in the war against Ayatollah Khomeini's Iran that had begun three years ago. Iran was showing no signs of retreat. The attack was so strong that it appeared that Iraq would have to back off. It was exactly then that the US envoy reached Iraq to provide reassurance and financial aid from behind the scenes.

On 20 December 1983, Saddam Hussein deliberately met the US President's envoy in front of the press and the glare of cameras. He was sending a clear message to the world, 'America is with me!' It was meant to be a clandestine meeting, but Saddam didn't want to keep it that way. He knew very well that he was putting the US in an embarrassing position, but he still went ahead and embraced the envoy and shook hands with him in front of the national and international press.

78　US Congressional Record: 20 September 2002 (Senate), pp.: S8987–S8998.

The US envoy was none other than Donald Rumsfeld. He was not a part of the government at that time but Ronald Reagan had chosen him as the emissary to Baghdad. All three key actors in this play were whimsical and unpredictable, and the combination worked well. It was during this meeting in Rumsfeld's presence that Saddam was alleged to have been handed over chemical weapons. Rumsfeld and Reagan were well aware of the kind of person Saddam Hussein was and how his hands and indeed every cell of his body were soaked in the blood of common people. The US knew that the lives of lakhs and lakhs of innocent citizens were in danger. But this wasn't a deterrent.

The US was still smarting from the wounds inflicted by Iran's Khomeini. The cleric and political leader had delivered a hard blow by uprooting the reign of Shah Mohammed Reza Pahlavi, who danced to American tunes. Furthermore, Khomeini kept the fifty-two diplomats of the American embassy in Tehran under house arrest for 444 days between 1979 to 1981 just to ensure that they remained in custody until the US elections. Reagan, scared of losing the vote, tried his best to pacify Khomeini but didn't succeed and the US continued to distrust the Iranian leader. Moreover, the Americans were losing sleep over what would happen if Khomeini succeeded in defeating Saddam and taking over Iraq. The Shia Khomeini was also a threat to the Sunni Saudi Arabia. All these were oil-rich nations and the US could not afford to have an enemy regime gaining power in the region. In other words, either Saddam had to win, or better still, Khomeini had to lose!

The US realized this wasn't possible with the military power that Saddam Hussein had at the time, and President Reagan promptly put Rumsfeld in charge of providing all necessary support to correct this situation. Rumsfeld is believed to have played a key role in the whole matter. Soon, Iran came under the surveillance of US satellites and detailed information about Iran's army and its movements were passed on to Saddam Hussein. Massive military aide was sanctioned for Iraq that included supercomputers. Saddam could make use of them to develop his own nuclear weapons. There were Howitzer guns, ammunition and helicopters. This was the usual stuff, but there was also a special parcel marked 'Handle with care' in bold letters, addressed to the 'Iraqi atomic energy commission'. Everyone felt that these parcels contained uranium and material for producing atom bombs, but it was only a facade. The parcel actually contained bacteria that could spread epidemics of plague, anthrax, gangrene and several other serious illnesses. It is believed that Rumsfeld had travelled to Baghdad to personally inform Saddam Hussein about the 'special shipment'. The supply continued for five years following that meeting to help Saddam stay in charge.[79]

The deceit was that all this was done by the commerce department because the Pentagon, America's defence establishment, was against the supply. In fact, in the consignment, along with chemical weapons were atropine injectors that could be used as antidotes. The Pentagon removed them from the consignment as they were against the antidotes being delivered to Saddam Hussein.[80]

---

79   Julian Borger, 'Rumsfeld "Offered Help to Saddam"', *The Guardian*, 31 December 2002: 'In December Mr Rumsfeld, hired by President Reagan to serve as a Middle East troubleshooter, met Saddam Hussein in Baghdad and passed on the US willingness to help his regime and restore full diplomatic relations'; Michael Dobb, 'U.S. Had Key Role in Iraq Buildup', *Washington Post*, 30 December 2002: 'Although U.S. arms manufacturers were not as deeply involved as German or British companies in selling weaponry to Iraq, the Reagan administration effectively turned a blind eye to the export of "dual use" items such as chemical precursors and steel tubes that can have military and civilian applications. According to several former officials, the State and Commerce departments promoted trade in such items as a way to boost U.S. exports and acquire political leverage over Hussein.'

80   Ibid.

The US was fully aware of how Saddam was going to use the technology they were providing. He actually began using chemical weapons right in front of America's eyes. It was unbelievable to see all that it tolerated for this man!

In one instance, one of Saddam's rockets fell on the USS *Stark*, docked in the Persian Gulf. Thirty-seven US Navy marines were killed. It was poetic justice that Saddam had received these rockets from the US as part of military aid. Despite losing its own marines, America didn't raise a word against Iraq and chided Iran instead, saying, 'Saddam is forced to attack indiscriminately because of you.'

Later, the US sent troops to the Gulf with the express purpose of destroying Iran's oil lines. It had only one strategy and hope while doing all this: Saddam would surely come in handy sooner or later. A section of the American administration which included Donald Rumsfeld had begun to see a reflection of Egypt's Anwar Sadat in Saddam. The US was under the impression that Saddam too would be a modern-day Islamic puppet like Sadat and this was the hope with which they expanded their footprint in the Gulf.

In 1988, the US army downed a passenger airbus plane in Iran, and close to 290 people lost their lives as a result. Khomeini was rattled to the core at that point. If the situation was restricted to Saddam Hussein alone, it would have been easy to handle, but the US had begun to fight on his behalf. He had support from other quarters as well, such as Soviet Russia. France too was in support and had disregarded the UN and other international organizations and helped Saddam create a massive atomic arsenal.

Khomeini must have realized that it would not be possible for him to fight such a strong opposition and that was why he stopped the fight within a week of the Iranian airbus attack.

This was a victory for the US, but Saddam felt that it was he who had made it happen and began to gloat. But the US was least interested in what Saddam felt and its objective was crystal clear:

business! As long as it could get that without effort, there was no need to continue humouring Saddam. That was why an entire division of the US political establishment entered Iraq under the leadership of Senator Bob Dole. He had a single-point agenda: to see how US companies could get more and more business contracts in Iraq.

Saddam had in fact started a period of the most cruel and despicable bloodshed and genocide in modern history. The Kurds of Iraq were facing death as Saddam used extremely toxic chemical weapons to exterminate thousands of them. The US turned a blind eye to all the atrocities and continued to supply chemical weapons to him.

We hardly have any opinions about the Kurdish people but we do have a lot of compassion for the Palestinians fighting for their motherland, or the Jews. We are apathetic when it comes to the Kurds. In fact, their fight is also for their motherland, and they far outnumber the Palestinians. Their demand is straightforward and simple: 'Give us an independent country of our own, even if it is small, but give us one.' The Kurds have been fighting for almost a century.

After the First World War, the then US President, Woodrow Wilson, had publicly given his word for the creation of Kurdistan. An agreement to the effect was signed in 1920, but the victorious Americans felt it was more important to convince the Turkish leader Kemal Pasha than to keep the promise given to the Kurdish people. The reason was that the powerful countries were eyeing the Ottoman Empire that was on the brink of collapse, and nobody paid any attention to the Kurds and their fight. They were spread across four countries: Turkey, Iraq, Iran and Syria. If an independent Kurdistan was to be formed, it had to be done by carving out small parts from all four countries. In reality, even this allocation and division was done by outsiders. Because according to the Treaty of Lausanne, Kemal Pasha rejected the demand for Kurdistan and ordered the Kurdish people to be distributed in the four countries. Pasha was known to be a reformist, but was no different when it came to the Kurds.

He banned Kurdish organizations and associations and refused to give them an independent nation and identity. Later, during the Second World War, Soviet Russia extended a hand of friendship towards the Kurds in Iran. The first independent Kurdish province took birth as the Kurdish Republic of Mahabad. But within a short period, Iran squeezed the life out of the nation soon after the independent Kurdish government had been established. The Kurdish dream of having a country remained unfulfilled.

The Kurds had hoped that their dreams would get wings after Saddam came to power in 1979. But Saddam had held on to the reins of power since 1968. His Bath party had signed a treaty with the Kurds in 1970 to give the Kurds political independence, though limited. This led the Kurds to believe that sooner or later their dream would come true. Saddam also allowed radio programmes to be aired in the Kurdish language, reaffirming the Kurds' belief that they would succeed.

But once Saddam became firmly established as the ruler of Iraq, he changed his tune. There were oil reserves in the region where the Kurds lived and Saddam's plan was to drive them out and gain control of them. He began relocating Arabs from other provinces in Iraq and settling them in the Kurdish region. This led to a conflict between the Kurdish forces and the Iraqi army in 1974. Realizing that the conflict would continue for a long time, close to 1.5 lakh Kurds fled to Khomeini's Iran, which peeved Saddam no end. His army bulldozed through Kurdish villages and ousted people from their homes. Gradually, the strife worsened, and when war broke out between Iraq and Iran, the Kurds were the ones who suffered the maximum casualties. Saddam began proclaiming that the Kurds were more interested in saving their own lives and didn't care about their motherland, pointing to their taking refuge in the enemy country Iran. He declared the Kurds as traitors and soon began a campaign to uproot them completely.

If lakhs of people had to be exterminated at a time, conventional weapons would be of no use. Saddam found an effective alternative. He used chemical weapons openly for the first time on 16 April 1987 on the Kurds in Balisan village. A busload of Kurds were taken out of their village, sprayed with pesticides and killed like insects. Once Saddam was convinced that this method worked, the frequency and intensity of chemical weapon attacks picked up pace. He started a new campaign called 'Al Anfal' which was aimed at annihilating the Kurds.[81] He handed the reins of the campaign to his brother, Ali Hasan Al Majid, who performed his duty faithfully and used chemical weapons with such a free hand that he began being called 'Chemical Ali'.[82]

'Chemical Ali', like Saddam, hailed from Tikrit. His work involved going from village to village on his motorcycle and delivering letters, but his fortunes changed once Saddam came to power. He became his right-hand man, like Heinrich Himmler was to Hitler during the Second World War. He looked just like Saddam Hussein, and it became easy for him to terrorize people. Once he was told to deal with the Kurds, he never looked back. His men would go from village to village, gather people, and separate the men, women and children, and the elderly. They would be loaded on to buses, and never be seen again. In several instances, they were made to stand on the edge of trenches, and Chemical Ali's soldiers would fire at them from behind. The dead would fall right into the trenches. This saved them the effort of disposing off many bodies.

81　　Adam Jones, ed., *Gendercide and Genocide*; Adam Jones, ed., *Genocide, War Crimes and the West*.

82　　*Independent*, 'Chemical Ali: The End of an Overlord', 25 June 2007.

Hundreds would be killed at a time, and the trenches would be covered with mud using bulldozers. Chemical Ali's favourite mode of killing was chemical weapons because it took hardly any effort and saved on ammunition! Chemical weapons were used to ravage village after village. Iraqi soldiers would enter a Kurdish village in the wee hours of the morning and spray the chemical weapons given by the US either from the borders of the village or from helicopters. The villagers would first get the smell of garlic, and soon enough go entirely silent.

On 16 March 1988, Chemical Ali's men attacked Habaza, a Kurdish village that the Iranian army had captured, with chemical weapons. When this village was visited by the Human Rights Watch organization soon after, their description was spine-chilling: 'Every being in the village lies lifeless ... some in fields, women near their hearth, children in courtyards, people in cars, drivers slopped with their heads on the steering wheels ... dead bodies scattered everywhere. Human Rights Watch researchers conducted interviews with dozens of victims, family members and eyewitnesses, and also examined documentary evidence and the exhumed remains of mass graves. The organization's website lists gory details of human rights abuse.

However, Saddam wasn't satisfied. When the US captured Saddam later, he did not express an ounce of remorse for the atrocities he had committed, and nor did Chemical Ali. When the case against him was on in court, the lawyer pointed at Chemical Ali and said, 'This man has killed close to 1.82 lakh Kurds.' In reply, the accused snapped at the lawyer, 'Don't inflate the figures; I have killed only 1.25 lakh Kurds.' This was a clear insight into his psyche. Later, the US got its hands on the recording of one of his speeches on radio. He was heard ordering his soldiers, 'Kill those Kurds ... not one Kurd should remain alive ... let me see who can stop us ... you don't worry ... especially about the international human rights organizations ... I will kill them.' With him being hanged on 25 January 2010, the era of the modern-day monster, Chemical Ali, had ended.

But the bitter truth was that the US had had no intentions of capturing either Chemical Ali or Saddam Hussein. It was more interested in controlling Khomeini using Saddam. This blind passion was so strong that in March 1986, when the United Nations Security Council brought out a resolution prohibiting Iraq from using chemical weapons, the US shot it down. Foolishly, Britain gave its support. With the exception of these two countries, the remaining members were of the opinion that there should be at least some protest or opposition to Saddam. The shamelessness of the international community was such that within two months of the resolution, the US itself sent a cache of seventy cartons of biological weapons to Iraq, of which twenty-one were of anthrax along with the botulinum toxin.

The very next year, in March 1987, the US's Contra affair was revealed. It had to accept that under this pact, it had promised to send Iran weapons in exchange for the release of the US diplomats held hostage in the embassy for 444 days. This meant that on one side, the US was blatantly sending biological and chemical weapons to Saddam's Iraq, and on the other sending ammunition to Saddam's arch enemy, Iran's Ayatollah Khomeini. All this information spilled out but it made no difference to US policies.

In May 1988, when Chemical Ali was using chemical weapons against the Kurds in Iraq, the US sent mustard gas to Saddam Hussein. This caught the attention of the world, and in August 1988 the United Nations Human Rights Commission passed a resolution against him. But the US stronghold was such that the resolution was defeated by a margin of 11 to 8, which meant no prohibition was sanctioned on Saddam. Some Scandinavian countries, European organizations and the Socialist International voted for the resolution against Saddam and at least upheld human values.

It was not a pure coincidence that in the same month Saddam opened a new front against Iran, openly using nerve gas, mustard gas and other poison gases in the attacks. Meanwhile, the US army brazenly began to fight on Saddam's side, making him four times stronger and so forceful that a staggering 65,000 Iranians lost their lives. Iran realized at that point that it was not possible for it to fight Saddam, who had thrown all rules to the wind, and who had the US support. Khomeini had to retreat, and a truce was called between Iraq and Iran.

This gave Saddam an opportunity to focus on the Kurds. Within a week of the ceasefire, in August, he sent helicopters to rain chemical weapons on Kurdish villages. The US was so pleased with Saddam that it sent him another parcel of botulinum and anthrax in September. At the same time, US Deputy Foreign Minister Richard Murphy defended America's actions, saying, 'America and Iraq's friendship is very crucial for long-term economic and political objectives.' Companies like Dow Chemicals soon proved how crucial they were—this particular one sold extremely toxic pesticides worth $1.5 million to Saddam Hussein, despite knowing very well who Saddam considered pests.[83] The *London Times* too reported in detail about how US chemical companies sold several dangerous chemicals including cyanide to Saddam in the latter half of the 1980s.[84]

---

83   Julian Borger, 'Rumsfeld "Offered Help to Saddam"', *The Guardian*, 31 December 2002: 'Furthermore, in 1988, the Dow Chemical company sold $1.5m worth (£930,000) of pesticides to Iraq despite suspicions they would be used for chemical warfare'; Susan Webb, 'Why the U.S. Concealed Its Chemical Weapons Role in Iraq', Peoplesworld.org, 20 October 2014. Many others, including *The Washington Post*, have reported about Dow's supply of chemicals to Saddam.

84   Judith Miller, Stephen Engelberg and William Broad, *Germs: Biological Weapons and America's Secret War*, pp. 98–123, 211, 253.

The US continued to expand Saddam's military might. On 25 July 1990, the US ambassador to Iraq, April Glaspie, met Saddam Hussein.[85] Around that time, Saddam had signed a peace treaty with Iran, the Soviets had withdrawn troops from Afghanistan, the Berlin Wall had fallen only the previous year, and the Cold War had ebbed. In these circumstances, Saddam was accumulating his troops on the Kuwait border. While people were looking for a few moments of peace, Saddam was busy creating a new problem. According to him, 'While Iraq was embroiled in its war with Iran, Kuwait had stolen massive amounts of Iraqi oil. And when we needed money for rebuilding our country, Iran and to some extent Saudi Arabia deliberately produced excess oil and brought down the global market price of oil. That is why Kuwait needs to be punished.'

Kuwait had been a part of Iraq till very recently, but it became an independent country with the end of the British protectorate. Saddam wanted to avenge this historical event, and that was the political reason for his attack on Kuwait. The other reason was commercial. Saddam needed a lot of money during the war, and that was provided by Saudi Arabia, which gave Saddam a loan of almost $26,000 million. It is believed that due to Saddam's war, Ayatollah Khomeini, the thorn in the flesh of the Shias and the royals, would be removed once and for all. Khomeini was becoming more powerful by the day. But Saddam changed his mind and refused to return the money to Saudi Arabia. He said, 'Because I crushed the Ayatollah's sting, the Saudis have benefitted; why are they asking for money back?' Seeing that not paying the Saudi debt and capturing Kuwait was a possibility, Saddam made his move and lined up his troops at the border.

Ambassador April Glaspie went to meet him under these circumstances. She told Saddam that the US was interested in

---

85   Stephen M. Walt, 'WikiLeaks, April Glaspie, and Saddam Hussein', *Foreign Policy*, 9 January 2011.

broadening and deepening its relationship with Iraq. Details of that meeting were released from government archives just recently, with the *New York Times*, *Washington Post* and other newspapers publishing them. According to reports, Glaspie had told Saddam, 'In fact, America as a policy does not interfere in the border disputes between two friendly countries. We have no opinion on the Arab–Arab conflicts, like your border disagreement with Kuwait. But we feel it is not right for you to have accumulated such a large number of troops at the Kuwait border.' Saddam smiled in response. She continued, 'I am giving you our Foreign Minister James Baker's message: "America has nothing to do with the Kuwait issue and it has no connection with America's relationship with Iraq."' This was America's unequivocal message during the meeting on 25 July 1990. On 2 August, Saddam's army entered Kuwait. He had taken over Kuwait within two days and appointed his brother Chemical Ali as the governor.

Excerpts from the Iraqi document on the meeting, published on 23 September 1990 in the *New York Times*, quote Glaspie as saying: 'I admire your extraordinary efforts to rebuild your country. I know you need funds. We understand that and our opinion is that you should have the opportunity to rebuild your country. But we have no opinion on the Arab–Arab conflicts, like your border disagreement with Kuwait. I was in the American Embassy in Kuwait during the late 60s. The instruction we had during this period was that we should express no opinion on this issue and that the issue is not associated with America. James Baker has directed our official spokesmen to emphasize this instruction.'

It continues: 'In a now famous interview with the Iraqi leader, US Ambassador April Glaspie told Saddam, "We have no opinion on the Arab–Arab conflicts, like your border disagreement with Kuwait." The US State Department had earlier told Saddam that Washington had "no special defense or security commitments to

Kuwait." The United States may not have intended to give Iraq a green light, but that is effectively what it did.'[86]

Some people opine that this meeting was to deceive Saddam. His perception after it was that America would not touch them irrespective of whatever they did. A few years later, a couple of British reporters questioned Glaspie regarding the matter and she responded squarely, 'We foolishly did not realize that Saddam was stupid. We didn't realize that he would interpret our words that way.'

The US had to do something, because had Saddam captured Kuwait, his next target would have been Saudi Arabia, which would not have stood a chance against Saddam's might. Imagine the situation if Saddam had got control of both Kuwait and Saudi Arabia! The three top oil-rich countries in the world would have come under Saddam's ownership, and he would have controlled 40–45 per cent of the oil production in the world. He would have literally made the world dance to his tunes!

If nothing else, the US understood the language of oil really well, especially with the 'oil-language' expert George Bush Sr coming to power. Bush wanted the US to intervene, but why it should have got involved in the dispute and gone to war was beyond the comprehension of ordinary US citizens.

Meanwhile, Kuwait was struggling to survive, and there was no sign of the US warming up for the war. Kuwait finally drew out its most potent weapon: money. It poured in the dollars—like anything can be bought with money, anything can be sold with money as well. Kuwait sold its war to the US, which hired its most prestigious and expensive PR company, Hill & Knowlton, for $12 million. The company sold the idea of the war to the American media, senators, Amnesty International, etc., through a campaign called Citizens

86   Stephen M. Walt, 'WikiLeaks, April Glaspie, and Saddam Hussein', *Foreign Policy*, 9 January 2011.

for a Free Kuwait. The objective of the national campaign was to raise awareness in the US about the dangers posed by Iraqi dictator Saddam Hussein to Kuwait. They spread a few true but mostly cooked-up stories of his atrocities. Amnesty International later accepted that most of the stories were imaginary.

As John MacArthur details in his book *Second Front: Censorship and Propaganda in the 1991 Gulf War*, a report titled 'Who Truly Was the Most Dishonest US President?' released as recently as 7 March 2021, 'An organisation calling itself Citizens for a Free Kuwait (financed by the Kuwaiti government in exile) had signed a $10m contract with the giant American public relations company, Hill & Knowlton, to campaign for American military intervention to oust Iraq from Kuwait. The Human Rights Caucus of the US Congress was meeting in October and Hill & Knowlton arranged for a 15-year-old Kuwaiti girl to tell the babies' story before the congressmen. She did it brilliantly, choking with tears at the right moment, her voice breaking as she struggled to continue. The congressional committee knew her only as "Nayirah" and the television segment of her testimony showed anger and resolution on the faces of the congressmen listening to her. President Bush referred to the story six times in the next five weeks as an example of the evil of Saddam's regime. The story was a fabrication and a myth, and Nayirah, the teenage Kuwaiti girl, coached and rehearsed by Hill & Knowlton for her appearance before the Congressional Committee, was in fact the daughter of the Kuwaiti ambassador to the United States. And her story was completely baseless.'[87]

---

87   Phillip Knightley, 'The Disinformation Campaign', *The Guardian*, 4 October 2001: By the time MacArthur revealed this, the war was won and over and it did not matter any more'; 'The Kuwaiti government-in-exile promptly hired a US public relations firm, Hill & Knowlton, whose Washington DC office was run by Bush's former chief of staff. The PR firm coached a purported witness, introduced

All these measures had the desired effect and a wave of opposition rose against Saddam in the US. President Bush grabbed the opportunity and decided to send US troops to save Kuwait. However, it must be said that though there have been innumerable reports about this PR agency, it would be incorrect to blame the US directly. Nevertheless, it needs to be mentioned that the Kuwait government in exile did have tacit US support.

An important event took place at this point, which possibly has repercussions to this day. The US army needed a military base in the area if they had to protect Kuwait. The Diego Garcia Island in the Indian Ocean was a little too far. Hence, the US requested Saudi Arabia to allow it to set up a military base there. Saudi Arabia was caught between the devil and the deep sea. On one side was Saddam's threat—and Saudi Arabia had sought US help against Saddam—and on the other was the dilemma of allowing US forces to land on Saudi soil. A young cleric went to King Fahd with a plea: 'This is the holy land of Mecca–Medina; please don't allow the Americans to set foot here. Our religion will perish.' The king asked, 'All that is fine, but how can I protect my reign? If I don't protect my throne, how will I protect my religion?' The cleric had an answer for that too. He said, 'Don't worry. I have a corps of fanatic Mujahideens ready. We will handle Saddam, but please don't allow America to come here.' King Fahd seemed to be convinced initially. That young cleric was none other than Osama Bin Laden.[88]

---

as a 15-year-old girl called "Nayirah", to tearfully tell US congressmen in October 1990 that Iraqi soldiers had entered a hospital in Kuwait, removed babies from incubators and left them to die on the cold floor. Nayirah, reporters were assured, was using an assumed name for fear of reprisals against her family back home. Only after the war would it emerge she was the daughter of Kuwait's ambassador to the US.'

88   Steve Coll, *The Bin Ladens: An Arabian Family in the American Century*; Adam Robinson, *Bin Laden: Behind the Mask of the Terrorist*.

Just a year ago, his Mujahideens had forced the Russian army to withdraw its troops from Afghanistan. He was still intoxicated by that success and believed that after the Russians, Saddam shouldn't be a big challenge. But what really happened after that meeting is known only to King Fahd and no one else. After momentarily being convinced, the king changed his mind about using Osama against Saddam and instead allowed the US to use Saudi soil for a military base. Osama would never have agreed for one Muslim nation to support the Israel backers to fight another Muslim nation. He was enraged by what happened and called for a jihad against America and all nations supporting it. It stands till date.

In reality, a lot of West Asian scholars have proven that the threat of Saddam targeting Saudi Arabia soon after his attack on Kuwait was a false alarm raised by America. The then American Secretary of Defense, Dick Cheney, showed the Saudi royal family satellite pictures of the troops that Saddam had readied on the Kuwait border. But later, the *St Petersburg Times* bought these images from the satellite company and revealed that the US had morphed the pictures to pressurize the Saudis. Following this revelation, several people tore apart President Bush's claim of Saddam's attack on Saudi Arabia. But it did give the US an opportunity to create a wave in favour of the Kuwait war. President Bush sent a large number of US forces to the Gulf and freed Kuwait, pushing Saddam back to Baghdad.

But the US did not have an answer for why its soldiers didn't oust him from power or kill him right away when he was cornered. The US had sent close to 7 lakh soldiers to Kuwait. Bush Sr could have done then what his son did ten years later. But he did nothing. When Secretary of Defense Dick Cheney was posed this question, he replied, 'If we had done something like that there would have been widespread manslaughter, and America would have been stuck in Iraq for a long time.' The US took a diametrically opposite stance

in 2003 and declared war to overthrow Saddam Hussein. But the
Americans who entered Iraq in 2003 couldn't exit till 2010.

The war was so intense that George Bush Sr could have finished
off Saddam and earned laurels. The 6,97,000 soldiers who fought
in it were gripped by a condition called the 'Gulf War syndrome'.[89]
It was a disease they caught from facing the chemical weapons used
in the war. It affected not only the body but the mind as well, and
many suffered psychosomatic disorders. It was caused by several
chemicals like pyridostigmine bromide that the US used during the
Gulf War as a pretreatment to protect troops from the harmful effects
of nerve agents. It was also caused by organophosphate-containing
pesticides; vaccines against anthrax; the toxic chemical sarin; and the
smoke from the Iraqi stocks of chemical weapons that the Americans
burnt, apart from other chemicals that Saddam's army used. Every
one of these played a role in the spread of the condition and caused
a variety of deleterious effects on US soldiers. Some lost their
memory, some suffered incessant headaches, some lost their power
of digestion and several suffered arthritis. All of them lost control
over their own muscles. There were cases of tumours, serious wounds
and nervous system damage. What the soldiers suffered after they
returned home was even worse. Their children were born disabled—
observed equally among male and female marines returning from
Iraq. Many US medical institutions and social organizations have
since published reports about the Gulf War syndrome, most of them
blaming Saddam Hussein's chemical arsenal for it. But weren't they
aware that it was the US which supplied these weapons to Saddam
in the first place?

The US tried to pump its fists after the hanging of Saddam
Hussein, and the blood on its hands went unnoticed for some time.
Quite a few other countries had an equal role to play in Saddam's

---

89   Frances M. Murphy, 'Gulf War Syndrome', *British Medical Journal*,
     1999, https://www.ncbi.nlm.nih.gov/pmc/articles/PMC1114762/

sins and atrocities,[90] such as Singapore, the Netherlands, Spain, Luxembourg, Egypt, and even India!

India had helped Saddam produce chemical weapons during his fight against Iran,[91] providing Iraq with several intermediates needed for the production of tabun, sarin and mustard gas. According to reports, India sent 60 tons of thionyl chloride and 2,343 tons of other chemicals to Iraq. Thionyl chloride is an important intermediate in the production of mustard gas. It was sent to Iraq officially labelled as a chemical used in the manufacture of pesticides. But Saddam used it for ulterior motives. India tried to defend itself, saying things like: 'What could we do? We rationalized our actions through raids, but naturally no one believed our claims.' This was also because the US did not trust India's chemical industry and its capabilities. It cautioned India to tighten its export rules, but to no avail. At one time, the chemical trade was happening on such a large scale that the US secret service blocked Indian ships carrying chemicals to Iraq midway and sent them back.

However, all these details came out only after the wounded American soldiers filed a suit against their own government. An Indian company was also named in the report. On 18 January 2003, CNN telecast a detailed programme after interviews with companies associated with the case. However, Saddam was India's friend at that time and stood in its support at various international forums, including the UN. But such political and international favours are never free.

---

90   John King, 'Arming Iraq: A Chronology of US Involvement', Iran Chamber Society, March 2003; Murray S. Waas and Craig Unger, 'In the Loop: Bush's Secret Mission', *The New Yorker*, 25 October 1992.

91   India maintained its stand against chemical weapons. But there were reports about India-based private companies' involvement in helping Saddam.

The matter exploded so violently that the US, despite having paid such a heavy price—human and financial—to find Saddam's WMDs in the form of chemical and biological weapons withdrew from the treaty banning such weapons. Once Saddam Hussein was completely annihilated, it recalled its representative from the Chemical Weapons Convention, resulting in the breakdown of the talks in Geneva. The US stated that it would 'come out with a new draft and take part in the talks' but nothing like that ever happened. On the contrary, it made a lot of excuses like how the present treaty gives a raw deal to European countries and is unfair to several others, and to this day maintains that a new treaty needs to be formulated.

Discussions on such a treaty have been ongoing since 1972, around which time an all-inclusive blueprint was put in place. This Biological Weapons Convention was recognized by 143 countries, all of which endorsed that the manufacture, development and production of biological weapons must be prohibited. But it remains a spineless declaration on paper, with all the developed countries among the signees continuing to ensure that it is never implemented and followed, similar to the treaties related to climate change and environmental protection. Everyone is aware that global warming needs to be controlled, but the US tells third-world countries to find their own solutions, reduce the use of cars and air conditioners, and plant trees, without pointing fingers their way. It is the same with biological weapons. The rules don't apply to all equally.

We are unable to fathom the extent of the damage this two-faced and hypocritical approach has caused. Such weapons that were owned by a few nations have now reached the hands of terrorist organizations, anarchists and even religious fanatic groups. If someone around us dies suddenly under mysterious circumstances of some unknown disease, it is quite possible that biological weapons or their components could be the reason.

We need to take care. Such incidents have started to happen around us.

11

Someone Is Out There!

THE most annoying aspect about large cities is that people living there have an abundance of everything, except time and space. Georgi Markov, BBC reporter in London, faced the same problem as he tried to navigate the rapid pace of life as a reporter, that too in London, where finding a place to live and space to park is a tough task. On 7 September 1978, he was about five minutes late reaching his office, by which time the parking lot of the BBC office was full.

Markov was an author and playwright, originally from Bulgaria, who raised voices of dissent against the communist Bulgarian regime. He and several others of his ilk had become a nuisance for the government. A large section of the leftist government that spoke the language of human rights came down heavily on protesters demanding freedom of speech and expression. One by one, they all left Bulgaria and sought refuge in London, where they were welcomed with open arms. Georgi Markov was among them. He made London his adopted motherland in 1969.

When he did not get a parking space that morning, he did not lose his cool. He reversed his car, turned to the right and reached Waterloo Bridge, where he found a parking space by the banks of the Thames River. The breeze blowing in from the cool, serene waters of the Thames calmed his mind as he walked happily towards his office, where he was head of the Bulgarian service of the BBC. As he walked, lost in thought, his pace was disturbed by a sharp prick in his thigh. He turned around to see an old man bending down to pick up his umbrella from the ground, mumbling, 'I am sorry.' It was possibly the tip of the umbrella that hurt him.

The same day, he developed a sudden fever and his blood pressure began falling. Medicines had no effect. His blood pressure became so dangerously low that the blood flow to his heart and brain literally stopped.[92] Nobody understood what was wrong, not even Markov himself. Except for the small prick from the umbrella that morning, nothing unusual had happened to him. The incident was so insignificant that he just made a casual mention of it to his wife.

He died the very next day. His sudden death became big news, especially in Bulgaria, where the newspapers spiced up the story and had a field day. Vladimir Kostov, who was also a Bulgarian journalist like Markov but in exile in France, read the news in Paris. He too had opposed the communist regime in his motherland. Kostov had faced experiences similar to Markov's. He too had fallen sick following a prick by a sharp object, exactly ten days before, when he was leaving a metro station. The same afternoon, he developed a high fever and his blood pressure became dangerously low. He was admitted to the hospital. Unlike Markov, his blood pressure rose gradually over the next five days and he survived. The moment he read about Markov's death, he was shocked enough to contact Scotland Yard and give

---

92   Robert Harris and Jeremy Paxman, *A Higher Form of Killing*, p. 200; Jeanne Guillemin, *Biological Weapons*, p. 138.

them the details of what had happened to him. The British police got to work.

Markov's dead body was X-rayed. Everything seemed normal, except for a spot on his thigh, where the umbrella had pierced his body. On closer investigation, they found that it was not just a spot but a tiny piece of metal lodged in his flesh, like the tip of a needle, hollow from the inside. Once they took it out and viewed it through a microscope, they found that the tip had four holes through which liquids could be injected. They investigated whether there was something similar stuck in Kostov's body too, and found what they were looking for to their shock. Poison was being released from the tip stuck in Kostov's body—a lethal poison named ricin. He was lucky that the dose calculation had gone wrong in his case and he survived.

It was a well-known fact that several countries had been trying to develop biological weapons using ricin, but no one had anticipated that it could be delivered so effortlessly. It happened so easily and stealthily in Markov's case that the needle of suspicion naturally pointed towards the KGB.

Bulgaria's communist President Todor Zhivkov was a puppet in the hands of the leftists, and the Bulgarian security services were being trained by the KGB. Doing away with enemies with such methods was part of their training.

There was a massive uproar regarding these two cases, and a lot of skeletons hidden in the cupboards of history came spilling out.

In February 1954, Captain Nikolai Khokhlov alighted in Frankfurt. He was sent by the KGB to supervise two other men whose task was to kill Georgiy Okolovich, chairman of the National Alliance of Russian Solidarists. On the day of the planned assassination, Khokhlov developed cold feet and instead told Okolovich that his life was in danger. He didn't stop there; committing treason, he went to the Americans and informed them about the assassination plot.

He took US officials to a forest and showed them a small pack of cigarettes kept hidden there. The packet was supposed to be given to Okolovich. If Khokhlov had lit the cigarette himself, he would have blown up in smoke because it contained an explosive material.

Captain Khokhlov shivered at the very prospect of killing someone like that. He later became a bitter critic of Soviet Russia and began delivering speeches against the regime all over the world. In September 1957, as he stepped down from a podium after a speech, in Frankfurt, he developed a high fever all of a sudden. His face turned blue-black, and a sticky substance began oozing from his eyes. Clumps of his hair began falling off. Doctors were certain that he would not survive, but the Americans wanted to keep him alive. They assigned a team of medical experts to monitor his health. They continued transfusing blood and pumping his body with steroids, cortisone and vitamins. The American doctors were interested in identifying what he was poisoned with. Khokhlov managed to survive. When the doctors analysed his blood samples, they found that Khokhlov was being fed radioactive substances with his food by the KGB!

Two years later, another Ukrainian rebel refugee, Stepan Bandera, died under similar suspicious circumstances in Munich.[93] He too was opposed to the Russian leadership. Bandera was considered the father of the Ukrainian nationalist revolution but was also a controversial figure. He was so against the Russians that he joined hands with the Nazis during the Second World War and guided Hitler's forces when they entered Ukraine. In 1941, he declared Ukraine an independent nation but later fell out with the Nazis. The Germans put him in prison in September 1941 after they became suspicious about Bandera's intentions. He remained in prison till the

---

93   Danylo Chaykovsky, 'Stepan Bandera, His Life and Struggle', http://
      exlibris.org.ua/murders/r04.html

end of the war. However, his activities didn't stop; his main agenda was to oppose the communist government. His opposition was so strong that the Soviets decided to finish him off. When Bandera returned home on the night of 15 October 1959 and opened the door, he turned around on hearing a sound. A man emerged and sprayed a chemical on Stepan's face. It turned out to be prussic acid, also called hydrogen cyanide. The moment this chemical comes in contact with the body, it goes into the lungs and makes the blood vessels constrict. The entire process happens so fast that the victim has no chance to save himself. The same happened with Bandera, and he died within seconds at the door of his house. Like in the case of Captain Khokhlov, nobody knew the reason for his death at that time. Those who poisoned him escaped from Ukraine after two years. When they spilled the beans, the world realized the levels to which chemical warfare had escalated.

A similar incident took place in 1964. West Germany was suspicious that its embassy in Moscow had been bugged because every word spoken there was reaching the Russian government. They combed the place and found cameras and microphones fixed in flower vases, fans, table-lamp switches, etc. These were only the ones they could spot. But there could be more such equipment that was unseen by the naked eye. Hence, the West German officials at the Moscow embassy called for technician Horst Schwirkmann, an expert in electronic devices, from their homeland.

He reached on a Sunday. Work would begin the following day. So, Schwirkmann decided to step out for a walk. As he was strolling around, he felt something prick him in the back. By the time he could register what it was, he had gone numb from the waist down and collapsed to the ground. The Germans rushed him to the US embassy and handed him over to the doctors there who were experts in treating chemical poisoning. The US had teams of such experts stationed at its embassies in communist countries.

On examination, they concluded that Schwirkmann had been poisoned with nitrogen mustard.

In several such cases, there were serious, visible, physical symptoms, but there were also a large number where the symptoms were mental. The most notable such instance took place in Hungary, a country caught up in the post–Second World War political realignment. It was firmly under Soviet control, and there was a lot of determined effort to free it from the stronghold. Cardinal József Mindszenty had become the face of the anti-communist revolt. He opposed the communists for restricting religious rights and freedom. Once the government realized that the revolt was going out of control, they arrested the cardinal and made him go on trial in Budapest.

By then, the cardinal's reputation had spread far and wide. Anticipating that he would give fiery speeches against the communists in the courtroom, thousands of people, including an army of reporters, began gathering there. But the picture was entirely different the moment he stood up to speak. He claimed to be in favour of the government and talked about how important it was for the Soviets to be present in Hungary. The journalists who were present in the courtroom that day reported that the cardinal's eyes looked lifeless, open but unseeing. It was as if his brain had lost control of his body. Several other people too made the same observation. Russia had developed a chemical using which they could control human minds, and their first test subject was Mindszenty. Later, US soldiers too had to face these chemical attacks during the Korean war. Several American soldiers captured by the Koreans had started to speak against their motherland. They began making statements about why the US should withdraw from that region. Following these incidents, the existence of such mind-controlling chemicals was confirmed.

Once a person consumes such a chemical, he becomes a robot. The CIA too procured these chemicals and the mystery behind

Frank Olson's death came to light. Many years later, in August 1977, the CIA admitted to such crimes. The US had undertaken 149 experiments in America to find ways to control the human mind. Close to 44 universities and colleges, 15 research organizations, 12 major hospitals and 3 prisons were assisting the CIA in these experiments. The matter didn't end here. The CIA used the American organization Society for the Investigation of Human Ecology as a front and provided grants for such experiments to various organizations in Britain, Canada, Finland, Israel and even Switzerland. Their attempt was to prepare a chemical for mind control before Soviet Russia could.

There were many such incidents during the post–Second World War and the Cold War era. During the Second World War, scientists tested ways of mixing female hormone Estrogen with food and giving it to Hitler on the sly.[94] Some scientists from the Allied countries had suspicions about Hitler's manhood, and the Office of Strategic Services—a precursor to the CIA—felt that Hitler straddled the 'male/female gender line' and therefore might easily be pushed towards one sex or the other. The head of the wartime research programme of the Office of Strategic Services, Stanley Lovell, focused his attention on Hitler's world-famous moustache. His idea was that if the experiment succeeded, Hitler's moustache would fall off and his voice would become feminine. Hitler would lose his confidence and it would be easy to defeat him. Lovell's team caught hold of Hitler's gardener. The plot was to mix female hormones with Hitler's food. Obviously, the conspiracy didn't succeed. The gardener took the money from the Allies, turned traitor and informed Hitler about the treacherous plots being hatched against him.

---

94 Robert Harris and Jeremy Paxman, *A Higher Form of Killing*, pp. 200–07; Stephen Adams, 'Revealed: Sex Hormone Plan to Feminise Hitler', *The Telegraph*, 14 August 2011..

The episode underscores the power of chemical and biological weapons. The US, Soviet Union and other factions had produced several such weapons. When the Second World War ended and the Cold War began, the hatred between the Americans and the Soviets reached unimaginable heights. In the 1980s, the Soviet Union propagated the news that AIDS was a disease created in America's laboratories.[95] Such news was spread for almost six years through Soviet-authorized newspapers and pro-Soviet media. Finally, the Soviet Academy of Sciences had to officially come out with a clarification in May 1987 that 'this was not true and AIDS was indeed a real disease and not created in laboratories'. The *New York Times* printed the news as bold headlines and the AIDS matter was cleared, but there are several other such matters that have not been revealed yet. The Cold War period was when new biological and chemical weapons came into being. But it was not only the US and the Soviets who were the culprits while all other nations were saints. The most mischievous was in fact South Africa.

Only Nelson Mandela and his struggle against Apartheid come to mind when we think of South Africa, but it is shocking to know the depths to which this conflict had reached. South Africa was desperately on the lookout for a vaccine during its research on biological weapons. Its political leaders wanted to have a vaccine at any cost, one that could render the recipient infertile for life. Its intended recipients were black Africans. The conspiracy was to have a yellow fever vaccination drive and instead inject the infertility chemical. Over a period of time, this would lead to a natural reduction in the black population in South Africa. There were also attempts to spread anthrax, Ebola and other diseases in black African communities.[96]

---

95   Jasmine Garsd, 'Long Before Facebook, the KGB Spread Fake News about AIDS', NPR, 22 August 2018.

96   Jan van Aken and Edward Hammond, 'Genetic Engineering and Biological Weapons', *Embo Reports*, 2003.

Once the racist regime fell, all these details were given to the fact-finding committee constituted by the new regime. It found twenty-two bottles full of cholera germs, huge cartons of chocolates mixed with anthrax and bolutinum toxin, cigarettes with anthrax germs and numerous crates of beer bottles contaminated with thallium. A lot of people lost their lives in the flames of racism, but there is no record of the number of people who lost their lives to man-made and human-controlled diseases.

Such efforts continue to this day. The freshest example of this is Alexander Litvinenko's wasting away to his death.[97] He was a former KGB officer who was annoyed with the exploitative systems that his rulers ran in the name of communism, and he switched sides, eventually settling down in London. His books that exposed the dark side of communism, *Blowing Up Russia: Terror from Within*, and *Lubyanka Criminal Group*, were bestsellers. In the first book, he gave detailed accounts of how the Russian secret services staged the Russian apartment bombings and other terrorist acts to bring Vladimir Putin to power. In the second, he gave shocking accounts of the bomb blasts carried out by the KGB in Moscow to defame the Chechen rebels and scare the Russians, the attacks on the Moscow theatre, the attack on the Armenian Parliament and other terrorist activities of the KGB. Litvinenko also mentions that when Osama Bin Laden's right-hand man Ayman Al Zawahiri visited Russia in 1997, he was given government security.

It was not surprising that Alexander Litvinenko had become a thorn in the Russian government's flesh. On 1 November 2006, he fell mysteriously ill. The best medical experts and teams of doctors tried to save him but all was in vain. He died after three weeks. His death in front of news cameras sent shivers all across the world.

---

97   Daniel Schorn, 'Who Killed Alexander Litvinenko?' CBS, 5 January 2007.

It had become clear that he had been poisoned with the radioactive element polonium. Litvinenko had gone for dinner with two KGB officers just a day before he took ill. The poisoning must have taken place during that meal. He recorded a statement before his death in which he openly accused Putin, 'It is time to give a piece of my mind to the person. You have succeeded in suppressing voices, but you have to pay the price for this forced silence sooner or later. Mr Putin, you might have silenced me, but the voices of dissent that will arise from far and wide will echo in your ears for a long time to come.'

Litvinenko died while Putin lost nothing.

The history of chemical and biological weapons is such. At the bottom of it all is a perverse hunger to search for the most toxic and lethal poison. A poison that will kill the victim and not leave a trace.

Many world leaders had made such attempts. Lavrentiy Beria was the crown prince of this gang. He was Soviet leader Stalin's right-hand man, so influential that Stalin took him along to the post–Second World War Malta conference where he introduced Beria to US President Theodore Roosevelt as 'our Himmler'. There is no match to the kind of atrocities Beria had committed. It is believed that this man poisoned even his leader, Stalin, who died on 5 March 1953. Beria had served him food four days before his death. Stalin fell sick the very next day and never recovered. Later, Beria too was killed during Krushchev's time. After his death, several stories emerged of his sexual perversion. Described as a 'sexual predator', Beria often would be driven in place of his stay, or even Moscow, in his military vehicle, and order his soldiers to pick up young girls and women. Even though Stalin was aware of his debauchery, he ignored it. But when he got to know that his daughter, Svetlana, was working with Beria on some task, he was shaken to the core! He immediately called her back and threatened her, saying, 'If you ever meet this man, beware!' This was a sample of Stalin's communism—one rule for his family and another for the masses.

The present form of biological and chemical weapons is worrisome. The fear is of the dangerous consequences of these weapons and the know-how falling into the hands of private operators, government-backed terrorist outfits and irresponsible administrations. But it appears to be too late.

When the Soviet Union disintegrated, the poison-manufacturing units became a part of these new nations, several of which supported Al Qaeda and the Taliban based on their religious affiliations. Fanatic Islamism and Islamic radicalization has spread over Kazakhstan, Tajikistan, Uzbekistan and many other nations.[98] The Hizb Al Tahir Islamia, Hizb un Nasrat, Islamic Movement of Uzbekistan, Tableek Jamaat and many other such Islamic fundamentalist organizations have sprung up in these regions. Osama Bin Laden and his associates decided to get involved, and several of them function as Al Qaeda divisions even today. This region around the Caucasus mountains is swarming with extremist fundamentalist organizations, and it is terrifying to even think of what will happen if chemical and biological weapons fall into their hands!

During the Cold War, the KGB hid its chemical and biological weapons in several European communist nations. The stores of such arms were for friendly nations, to be used whenever the need arose. The stocks in other countries were meant for internal use. What will happen to such stockpiles is a question that worries the intelligence services of several nations.

British intelligence agency MI5 has identified thirty-two spies of the Russian foreign intelligence service, the SVR, operating under full diplomatic cover from its London embassy in Kensington. The spies have links to former deep-cover KGB agents who, during the Cold War, hid scores of genetically engineered biological warfare

---

98   Zeyno Baran, S. Frederick Starr and Svante E. Cornell, 'Islamic Radicalism in Central Asia and the Caucasus', Central Asia-Caucasus Institute and Silk Road Studies Program, July 2006.

weapons in Britain's countryside.[99] Gordon Thomas, a political and investigative writer, wrote several accounts on the British and Israeli secret service, among them the bestselling book *Gideon's Spies*. According to an article he wrote in 2005, available on Centre Français de Recherche sur le Renseignement (CF2R), many former KGB agents are now working for the Al Qaeda. Not only that, but several KGB agents also who lost their jobs following the disintegration of the Soviet Union sold classified information regarding biological weapons for money, literally auctioning off the information to the highest bidder.

Alexander Kouzminov was at one time a senior KGB officer and the head of its ultra-secret unit Department 12. 'Our work was biological espionage, planning and preparation of acts of biological terrorism, sabotage and biological war,' he revealed. Now a resident of New Zealand and the author of the *Biological Espionage*, he made some claims that stunned the world. He revealed that the germs were created after the Soviet Union signed the 1972 Biological Warfare Convention. They were engineered in secret laboratories in the Ural Mountains, and from there the vials were smuggled into Britain in diplomatic bags. Scientists at Porton Down, Britain's biological defence establishment, fear the vials could contain plague germs and even smallpox. From Britain, these spread to other countries in Europe. Every word he has written has been found true and experts believe the reality could be far more serious. This can be borne out by what is known as 'the briefcase bomb'.[100]

On 12 September 2001, a day after the terrorist attack on the World Trade Center, an intensive search was in progress to detect nuclear devices allegedly hidden in the New York City area. No nuclear

---

99 Gordon Thomas and David Dastych, 'Dysfunctions: Bio-Roulette', Canada Free Press, 17 October 2005.

100 Ibid.

weapons had been found then, but four years later in 2005, the problem resurfaced and the discussions resumed. The serious issue was that, according to experts, apart from Al Qaeda, there could be Chechen rebels and other organizations from West Asia involved as well. Around the same time, the secret service agencies reported that Chechen rebels had sold twenty such briefcase bombs to Al Qaeda and that the latter had paid a hefty sum of $30 million for them. Paul Williams, author of 'Al-Qaeda: Anatomy of Terror' and investigative journalist writing on international terrorism, indicates the future terrorist attacks would be carried out with biological and chemical weapons. His opinion has been seconded by Theodore Taylor, a prominent American nuclear specialist.

What exactly is the briefcase bomb? It is basically a miniaturized nuclear weapon. Traditional nuclear bombs use radioactive uranium, plutonium and other such heavy metals, while the briefcase bomb has a chemical called red mercury. It is an extremely dense chemical which looks like squishy jelly, and its radioactivity is also relatively low. It is hence very difficult to detect and can be trafficked in a clandestine manner. It is being traded freely in the black market and can be procured easily for around $5 lakh per kg.

These facts came to light when the British police arrested in London four youth on 24 September 2004 from an undercover operator. Three of them had come to purchase red mercury while the fourth had come to guide them to the person who could provide them funds for the purchase. The shocking fact was that the funds were being provided by a wealthy Saudi Arabian whose name the British police never revealed. But the message from the episode is loud and clear.

The briefcase bomb is a kind of neutron bomb that produces nuclear radiation on explosion. It can emit intense thermal radiation, creating a fireball with a diameter that can expand to 460 feet. The core of the fireball could reach a maximum temperature of 10 million degrees Celsius. The heat that collapsed the World Trade Center towers on 11 September 2001 never exceeded 5,000 degrees Celsius. Nuclear briefcase bombs are obviously much more dangerous and could devastate all forms of life in the radius of a mile.

Porter Goss, the first director of the CIA, was reported to have said while making a statement to the House Intelligence Committee, 'It would be naïve to believe that terrorist organizations wouldn't have got hold of these new weapons.' Even Robert Mueller, the sixth director of the FBI, said, 'My greatest concern, Mr Chairman, is that our enemies are trying to acquire dangerous new capabilities with which to harm Americans. Terrorists worldwide have ready access to information on chemical, biological, radiological and nuclear—or CBRN—weapons via the Internet.'

What else should we worry about?

Mueller was talking about organized terrorism, and many nations hardly have a role to play in such matters except as victims to the attacks! As we speak, lethal chemical and biological weapons are being used at different levels. It is not only terrorists and political groups that are involved in this deadly business, but even spiritual groups and organizations.

We know that the former is undoubtedly dangerous, but what about the latter?

12

Beware of Such Gurus!

SHAKEY'S Pizza was a popular American restaurant in Dalles, Oregon, started by Dave and his wife, Sandy, post retirement. The restaurant's salads with fresh lettuce, cherry tomatoes, broccoli and olive oil were in high demand. The salad menu changed as per the season, but their quality and goodness remained unchanged. But the calm and convivial atmosphere[101] was shattered on 9 September 1984. For the first time, some local police officials had come there to take food samples for testing. That day, many diners had suffered such severe bouts of diarrhoea that they had to be hospitalized. When the police and local health officials came to investigate the matter, they ruled out the possibility of the owners' involvement because they too had been affected and were in the hospital.

The officials soon realized that this was not restricted to a single restaurant. The entire town had suffered a gastroenteritis epidemic,

---

101 Judith Miller, Stephen Engelberg and William Broad, *Germs*, pp. 15–25.

and close to 751 people had been affected. Fortunately, no lives were lost, though one woman went into premature labour because of the incident. People were terrified and there were worries about a law and order problem being created, and questions were raised about the state of the local health care system. The locals vented their anger on the doctors and complaints piled up at newspaper offices around town.

Municipal officials were hesitant because they couldn't announce that this wasn't an ordinary gastroenteritis epidemic. If they did, more questions would have been raised. The truth was that the doctors themselves had no clue. Only one man seemed to have a clue: Judge William Hulse. He had suffered similar symptoms a few days prior. An idea began to form in his head about what could have happened.

A large settlement had come up near the Wasco County of Oregon about four years ago. People from all over the world had made it their home—it was a closed community of sorts where the people grew their own food, ate and danced together. It was a confined place and the inmates had nothing to do with the areas nearby. But their contact with the town was established when the local elections were just a couple of months away. The members of the new settlement wanted to have their own representatives in the local elections, considering the large number of inmates who lived there. But the locals were not keen on the idea of giving political power to outsiders. The dispute heated up so much that the inmates of the settlement began to threaten the locals. The situation was getting out of control, and Judge William Hulse made a visit to check the size of the community and its activities. He parked his car and walked around it with his colleagues. As they were about to leave, they realized that one of their car tyres had got punctured. As they waited for it to be replaced, the manager of the community offered Judge Hulse a seat and something to drink.

The very next morning, Judge Hulse's stomach began to churn, and soon he had severe bouts of diarrhoea. He had to be hospitalized as his condition worsened. His blood pressure and blood sugar levels dropped drastically and his condition turned critical. But the doctors did their best and Judge Hulse's digestive system gradually stabilized. It took almost three weeks for the weakness to subside. Seeing the residents of his county face the same symptoms and illness, he was now sure of the source: Acharya Rajneesh.

The citizens of Pune were vexed with this guru, who offered his disciples the path to nirvana through sex. The collective nuisance of his disciples was giving the locals sleepless nights. The crowds of onlookers waiting to get a glimpse of such seekers of enlightenment swelled by the day and became a big hindrance for residents living in the area. There were complaints about Acharya Rajneesh and his disciples consuming prohibited drugs to reach their heights of bliss. The locality, Koregaon Park, had become a haven for drug peddlers. A wave of hatred rose against Acharya Rajneesh and his acolytes.

The guru then decided to move out of his motherland. Funds were never an issue. He had a fleet of thirty-eight Rolls Royce cars, gem-studded watches and innumerable sannyasinis or female disciples. He was on the lookout for a new paradise to move to with his retinue.

Ma Anand Sheela, who joined Rajneesh in 1989 as a replacement for Ma Lakshmi, was spearheading the entire move.[102] She told him, 'You look for a place to set up the commune in India and I will look for one in America.' Though Rajneesh did not have permission to go to the US, she also helped him get a visa on health grounds, saying he needed treatment for back pain!

---

102 Catherine Collins, 'Ma Anand Sheela: Media Power through Radical Discourses', in Andrew King (ed.), *Postmodern Political Communication: The Fringe Challenges the Center*, pp. 115–131.

Ma Anand Sheela first set up a makeshift commune called 'Chidvilas' in New Jersey. But there was not much scope for expansion because of its proximity to New York. They resumed their search for a new place, and it ended in Dalles. Ma Anand Sheela procured close to 64,000 acres of barren land in Wasco County for $6 million. The land was suitable for their purpose because the rules of the area regarding the entry of outsiders were not as stringent compared to other states. The land was also relatively cheaper and the closest city was Dalles, a two-hour drive away.

Acharya Rajneesh fell in love with the location. Slowly and steadily, an entire township took shape, neat rows of identical houses lined with trees and flowering plants. There were beautiful shopping malls, health care centres and hospitals. There was a hotel with 150 rooms; discos and casinos for the entertainment of the inmates once they came out of their meditation; a helipad to ensure that the guru was not disturbed by the movements and activities of ordinary mortals! To remind people that it was a spiritual place, there was a tabernacle or prayer house spread over 2 acres. The place was planned in such a way that once a person entered, he didn't have to step out for anything. The settlement called Rajneeshpuram was completely self-sufficient and self-contained.

The *New Yorker* wrote an article in 1983 detailing Rajneeshpuram. It said that there were fourteen irrigation systems installed in the commune, and its farms produced all the vegetables and fruits needed for the inmates. It also had dairy farms and produced its own electricity. There were eighty-five bus routes for internal travel and a telephone exchange. Ma Anand Sheela had set all this up. She was so ambitious that she had created her own security team—in some ways the guru was her prisoner. He was soon going to pay the price for not reining in the disciple who aspired to become the leader.

Initially, the locals were happy with the community of spiritual seekers because whenever the inmates stepped outside the commune, they spent a lot of money and helped the local economy flourish. Even otherwise, the people of Rajneeshpuram didn't cause any problems. Whatever they did was restricted to their commune. But the problems arose with Sheela's political ambitions. She wanted to set up her own institution in the name of Rajneesh, and he was merely an instrument for her mission. She was very clear about what she wanted and was happy every time Rajneesh was in his period of silence. That gave her a free hand to do as she pleased. When Rajneesh expressed his desired to break his vow of silence she would openly oppose him.

Sheela wanted to expand Rajneeshpuram, but her intentions were against the rules of the local administration. They refused to give her permission. So, instead of changing her plans, she decided to change the local government itself. For that, she needed two of the three representatives from Wasco County to be from her side. That seemed a tough ask in the circumstances as she did not have the support of the voters. In fact, Ma Sheela was exploring an alternative to garner the votes needed for her representatives to win, but she didn't want to spend time convincing ordinary voters. She wanted a quick-fix solution.

So, she decided to import voters. Sheela and her clique decided that they would register as many voters as possible from the commune for the elections in November 1984.[103] She started a campaign to provide shelter to all the homeless and destitute people from all over America. The volunteers went from town to town and brought such people to the commune at Rajneesh's expense. People from outside Oregon were in no position to see through their cunning ploy. They genuinely believed that the benevolent hermit was providing shelter to them. But the locals knew the reason for this large-heartedness

---

103 Judith Miller, Stephen Engelberg and William Broad, *Germs*, pp. 22–25; Sven Davisson, 'The Rise & Fall of Rajneeshpuram', Archives of Ashé Journal, Vol. 2, No. 2, 2003.

and complained to the government. Judge William Hulse and his colleagues then went to the commune for an enquiry.

Rajneesh's followers were looking at multiple strategies for the elections. If their voter-import strategy failed, they had an alternative in mind. When their voter-import plan was noticed by the government, the rules for voting were tightened. The Wasco County clerk countered this attempt by enforcing a regulation that required all new voters to submit their qualifications when registering to vote. This was going to prove a hindrance, but the commune still had Plan B in place—to ensure that the local voters were not able to exercise their franchise. Rajneesh's disciples and the commune leadership planned to incapacitate voters in Dalles, where most of the voters resided. This was how the first germ attack took place in the US—the single largest bioterrorist attack in US history.

The weapon of choice was a bacterium called Salmonella enterica typhimurium. It is capable of multiplying rapidly once it enters the human digestive tract, affecting the mucosal secretions of the intestine and the villi on the intestinal walls. The small intestine and the gullet become weak. Waves of thin fluids begin to get secreted, resulting in severe loose motions. Victims suffer headache, body ache and fever. Pregnant women, children and the elderly are severely affected. Such infections can be fatal. Another bacterium of the same species causes typhoid.

Once the root cause of the epidemic was clear after the restaurant incident, the organizations responsible for epidemic control got into action. All health care agencies focused on germ attacks took notice and began the fight to control the epidemic. That was when the ugly and frightening truth came out.

The key instigator was Acharya Rajneesh's top disciple, Sheela Silverman, christened Ma Anand Sheela by him. Born Sheela Ambalal Patel in Baroda, she was sent by her father to the US to study when she was eighteen. She ended up marrying American billionaire Mark Silverman from Illinois. At that time, a large number of Americans, disillusioned by the materialistic American life, were attracted to Indian religious gurus. The Silvermans were charmed by Acharya Rajneesh and moved to his Pune ashram, where she became Ma Anand Sheela in 1981 and made a place for herself in his inner circle. Soon, she became Rajneesh's personal assistant and earned so much trust that she was handed the reins of the ashram. It was her decision to set up the commune in the US. Despite claiming to be a spiritual person, she continued to be crass, rude and brazen, a fact remarked upon by a few reporters who interviewed her in the US and Australia. Her language was so crude that it shocked them.

Her partner in crime in the germ attack in Oregon was Diane Yvonne Onang, alias Ma Anand Pooja. She was a nurse practitioner and secretary-treasurer of the Rajneesh Medical Corporation, the commune's medical research centre. She and Sheela purchased Salmonella bacteria from a Seattle-based medical supply firm called the American Type Culture Collection Company. Such activities were otherwise banned in the US, but since the demand had come from a medical research facility, it was not refused. The bacteria vials reached the commune without a hitch.[104] The two women and eleven other assistants took good care of the bacteria and ensured that their numbers multiplied.

The bacteria were ready for use in August 1984. Twelve disciples did a reconnaissance and selected a few restaurants in the Dalles area that they visited frequently and where they had become acquainted with the chefs, waiters and other employees. Restaurants in the US are mostly self-service ones, especially salad bars, which made things quite convenient. The commune's disciples added bacteria into the

---

104 Judith Miller, Stephen Engelberg and William Broad, *Germs*, pp. 15, 18–33, 24, 26, 28; James S. Gordon, *The Golden Guru: The Strange Journey of Bhagwan Shree Rajneesh*.

salad ingredients as they served themselves. The very next morning, they heard about the success of their mission and were ecstatic. The same game was to be played on a larger and deadlier scale in November, just a day before the election.

However, these plans went haywire. The US government agencies did not give them a chance, and medical officials and a large posse of local police raided the commune. Their target was the medical research centre, where as expected they found large stores of Salmonella bacteria grown under controlled conditions in the state-of-the-art facility. The officials were shocked to also find large stocks of electronic espionage devices and spying equipment. They even discovered apparatus for testing lethal disease-causing germs, probably used on the homeless and destitute people brought there from different parts of the US. This was the first time such a large, private biological weapon-manufacturing unit had been exposed. The US administration was shocked and it ordered a detailed investigation into the matter.

The mayor of Rajneeshpuram, David Berry Knapp (Swami Krishna Deva), was arrested and interrogated by the police. Several others were also taken into custody, but they all remained tight-lipped. The police threatened Knapp, saying, 'You have two options; one is to give us all the information we want and get a pardon, or refuse and go to heaven with your partners in crime.' Knapp chose the former. From then on, it was easy going forward for the police.

According to him, the poisoning plan was the brainchild of Ma Anand Sheela and Ma Pooja. The moot point was whether Rajneesh was aware of the plan. Knapp said that Rajneesh cleverly confused everyone without uttering any falsehood. He would have agreed to everything if the plan conceived by his two disciples had succeeded, and backed off if it hadn't. Knapp not only spoke the truth unequivocally, but also gave the police recordings related to the episode that involved Rajneesh. In one tape, Rajneesh responds to a question from one of his female disciples, saying, 'There is nothing wrong in committing a few questionable actions to keep our ideology intact and spread it. Don't worry. I am there with you.' This was taken quite literally by the two disciples who engineered the poisoning act.

Whatever be the case, Rajneesh was not destined to succeed. Both his plans bit the dust just before the elections. Perhaps he forgot to advice the two 'Mas' on what to do if the police foiled their plans. The two of them disappeared the moment they saw the law tightening around them and escaped to Germany. They were nabbed on 28 October 1985 but couldn't directly be charged with using biological weapons because there were no such legal provisions in the US and Germany at that time.

The two were charged with attempting to murder Judge Hulse, and sent back to America. Both of them decided to plead guilty and were sentenced to anywhere between three to twenty years in prison under various sections of the law. But owing to good behaviour in prison, they were released after two years. Then both of them went to Switzerland, where Sheela married Swiss citizen Urs Birnstiel, a fellow Rajneesh follower, purchased two nursing homes and managed them. She continued to live in Switzerland after Birnstiel's death.

Rajneesh himself was under a vow of silence at that time, which he must have broken sometime around 16 September 1985 when he addressed a press conference. It had been a year since the Dalles poisoning and it was the first time he had spoken after the controversy. He shocked the world when he tried to wash his hands off, blaming the two women for whatever happened. According to him, both were vile and they never told him anything about their plans. 'They had plans to loot the commune. Not only did they plan to kill me, my female companions and two of my doctor friends, they also left a debt of $5.5 crore on my head. They were both fascists of the first order', he was reported to have claimed.'

But his tirade had no effect because his true colours had been exposed! The very next month, on 27 October, the police arrested him while he was attempting to get away from Oregon and leave the US. Within an hour of taking off from Oregon, the police forcibly made his plane land in North Carolina. There were not one or two but thirty-five criminal cases filed against him. He realized his game was over and pleaded guilty. He was fined $400,000 and sentenced to ten years in prison. More importantly, he was warned against setting foot in the US for the next five years.

Rajneesh was fortunate that there were no twenty-four-hour news channels at the time. Importantly, the US government too did not want this episode to get too much attention because they feared that it might inspire others to do similar things. The government itself was involved in the manufacture of biological weapons and it would not have been in their best interests to publicize this incident. It was worried that its cover would be blown. It went to the extent of requesting the reputed medical journal *Nature* not to publish its research findings related to this issue for at least three years. The journal acceded to the request.[105]

But clamping down on the voice of a magazine was not going to keep things under wraps. Far away in Japan, ten years after the Rajneesh incident, another self-styled guru was going to bite the dust.

19 March 1995 was a typical Monday, with people emerging from the lethargy of the weekend. In Tokyo, railway stations were spilling over with people rushing out of suburban railway stations to their offices. But that day, the moment they got off the trains, they smelt

---

105 OregonLive, '25 Years after Rajneeshee Commune Collapsed, Truth Spills Out', 5 February 2019.

something fishy. Soon, people began fainting. A few minutes later, the seriousness of the situation hit them. Close to a dozen people lost their lives, hundreds fell sick and thousands were injured in the resulting stampedes.

Cities across the world were stunned and shocked by the news—Japan had been attacked with poison gas, released into five local trains. Apart from those visibly affected, there were thousands who had invisible wounds. Prominent among them were two governments: the US and Japan. The former had suspicions that something like this could happen while the latter had never imagined that it could be a target of such an attack. When news of the attack reached the White House, it was received and taken note of by the national coordinator for security, infrastructure protection and counterterrorism, Richard Clarke.

He called up officials of the health department to discuss the next course of action. Even though it was Japan's problem, the Americans couldn't be certain that the same wouldn't happen in the US. The administration swung into action and called for a meeting of the security agencies. Experts in the field of chemical and biological weapons were invited to it. One thing was clear before a future course of action could be discussed—a religious cult, Aum Shinrikyo, was behind the Tokyo attacks.[106] The Americans were perplexed because they had never heard of it.

The mystery took the form of a mad dash as soon as CIA officials in Tokyo reported that 'the Aum cult' had an office in Times Square in New York, right at their doorstep.[107] After a lot of dilly-dallying, the officials decided to raid the Aum office in the middle of the night. But they were so naïve that they didn't bother to wear masks

---

106 Judith Miller, Stephen Engelberg and William Broad, *Germs*, pp. 151–54, 160–63, 190–93, 197–98, 202–03, 224.

107 Ibid., p. 153.

or take any precautions despite the chemical threat. Thankfully, nothing untoward happened. However, the visit only increased their worries because they found nothing apart from some pamphlets of religious teachings. The question that arose was: how could the Aum cult afford to rent an office in such an upmarket and expensive area of New York for their religious activities?

Shoko Asahara, the founder and head of the Aum Shinrikyo cult, was partially blind and had long hair. His eyes were half-closed like an ascetic. He must have been a complicated man because his thought process was influenced by Christianity, Buddhism, Hinduism and yoga, apart from Nostradamus. He had founded his cult as a mix of all these faiths and called it Aum Shinrikyo. 'Aum' means the same as in Hinduism, while 'Shinrikyo' stands for the 'ultimate truth' in Japanese. He declared himself a modern-day Christ, and was of the belief that he had been born to rid the world of sin and cleanse the black deeds of mortals.

This is true of most religious leaders. They declare themselves to be some incarnation or the other and get away by saying all kinds of things. Asahara was no different. He was trying a different trick, by telling people that doomsday was nearing and only the selected, pure souls would survive it to create a new world. The so-called selected ones were those who sang his praises. His cult grew bigger and bigger. British royals, Jews and Americans were enraged because Asahara brazenly claimed that they were out to divide the world.

He firmly believed that the US was going to attack Japan and cause the Third World War and a terrible nuclear war. His followers believed him blindly. But the 'guru' didn't do things for free. People had to pay hefty sums to be a part of his cult: 50,000 people from different parts of the world had paid fees to acquire his 'doomsday-protecting life jacket'. Soon, his net worth had soared to $1 billion. The organization that he had started from a small room teaching yoga and meditation went international within five years. Educated young men and women from Japan's universities became his followers.

Signs of what he would go on to do were clear but no one paid attention. Voices were raised against the Aum cult for the first time in 1993. That year, representatives of the cult approached a Middlefield, Connecticut, company for the purpose of purchasing an interferometer. The company sought permission for the sale from the US government because the export of the equipment was prohibited. Interferometers are sophisticated devices used to make critical measurements of polished surfaces using lasers, and have nuclear applications and in making bombs. The US government should have been alerted by the fact that a religious cult was ordering such equipment, but it took no notice.

Another incident took place a year later—a lethal sarin gas leak in the city of Matsumoto in Japan. Eight people were killed and over 500 harmed in the incident. US authorities were totally ignorant about it and CIA officials in Japan didn't even bother to report the matter to the US government. The Japanese government stated, 'A resident was believed to have accidentally released the gas while mixing a home-made batch of herbicide for his garden.' But the matter was not as simple as it was made out to be.

The media got suspicious, and two television channels came together and requested Kyle Olson, an American chemist, to investigate the incident and make a report. Olson provided the most accurate analysis of the Matsumoto incident, viewing it as the handiwork of unnamed terrorists. He said, 'It was physically impossible for the incident to be an accidental gas leak since none of the compounds found in the house could have caused the toxic results of the incident.' In addition, traces of sarin were found near the spot where witnesses had seen individuals in a vehicle releasing some type of gas. Olson realized it could merely be a dry run, and the next sarin attack would be in the Tokyo subway system. Other commentators too noted the interest of the Aum cult in sarin and clearly hinted that it may have been behind the Matsumoto incident.

The US government did nothing, but Olson was serious. He published pamphlets about the incident at his own expense and distributed them widely. Despite that, he wasn't taken seriously by the US media. Then the Tokyo attack followed and shook everyone out of their slumber. The followers of the Aum Shinrikyo cult shot dead the Tokyo city police officials who took action against the cult members. They killed one more person by giving him an overdose of a chemical agent.

Within a month of the Tokyo railway station attacks, on 19 April 1995, a terrorist attack took place at a government building in Oklahoma City in America. Over 200 people lost their lives and 168 were injured. One of the FBI officials investigating the incident found a film roll which indicated a chemical attack would shortly take place in Disneyland on Easter Sunday. There were also pictures of hands manufacturing chemical weapons.

Senior FBI investigating officer John Sopko got suspicious. 'These hands look like they belong to the Aum cult followers.' The basis for his suspicion was the Russian intelligence agency. Before the Aum Shinrikyo cult, the subject of Sopko's research was the alleged weakening control of Russia over its nuclear weapons. Sopko had reported to the American Congress, 'The Russian government does not care for its nuclear weapons and the people handling them. Those people are not given adequate salaries and facilities to live a comfortable life. This is potentially very dangerous because these men could sell nuclear technology and knowhow to international terrorist organizations just for money.' He had evidence to back his concerns because he had been in touch with premier scientific organizations in Russia. He had information which indicated that one of the international terrorist outfits trying to get hold of this technology was the Aum Shinrikyo cult.

After this information came out and the attacks in Tokyo happened, the security agencies of America and Japan went behind Shoko Asahara. The materials they found at several of his premises blew their minds! They found sarin gas stocks, biological weapons causing anthrax, plague, Q fever and several other diseases. The very thought of what would have happened if these were ever used sent a chill down the spine.

The Japanese government shut down and banned the Shinrikyo cult on 10 October 1995. All its assets were seized, and the cult declared bankruptcy the following year. The police arrested several people associated with it. There would be terror attacks in some place or the other in Japan whenever an official was caught. Shoko Asahara himself was arrested on 16 May 1995. The very next day, a letter bomb was delivered to the governor of Tokyo. The governor escaped unhurt but his secretary lost his fingers in the explosion that ensued. The police filed charges and Asahara was accused of manslaughter. Twenty-eight serious criminal cases were filed against him.

Despite Asahara's arrest, the cult continued its activities under another name. Today, the followers come together under the new name, Aleph. Asahara's disciple Fumihiro Joyu is its head.

In July 2000, the KGB arrested Dmitri Sigachev, a former KGB official. He and four of his colleagues were imprisoned because they were followers of the Aum cult and were planning attacks in some Japanese cities.

Lately, such religious cults are mushrooming everywhere and seem to be working in tandem. It is almost impossible to predict how and where the next attack will be. It's the common man who is left helpless and abandoned amidst all this.

13

Flow of the Genes

THIS has been the story of chemical and biological weapons and the search for answers to questions arising in this context. The biggest question that looms is regarding the future possibilities of their use. Some of these weapons are spread all over the ocean floor, some on islands and some in boats that have been sunk deliberately.[108] Some of these weapons float, get caught in fishing nets or reach the shores and find freedom.

It's not a one-off incident; but happening often since the Second World War. Once the war ended, Britain got back forty warships and loaded them with chemical weapons captured from the Germans. These were taken close to Norway in the northern hemisphere and blasted one after the other. The same was done in the Baltic Sea, where thousands of tons of chemical bombs lie settled on the seabed.

---

108 David Bearden, 'US Disposal of Chemical Weapons in the Ocean: Background and Issues for Congress', Library of Congress Washington DC Congressional Research Service.

The weapons lie there, waiting to be released. Britain didn't do this only with weapons captured from the Germans but also with those developed in their own country. The British have drowned 1 lakh tons of chemical weapon agents in the seas bordering Scotland.

The US is a step ahead. It did the same but not in their own waters. They drowned weapons captured from the Japanese in the Pacific Ocean surrounding South East Asia. Soviet Russia is the worst of the lot. They collected the mustard gas stocks captured from Germany, filled them in cylinders and loaded them into navy boats and dumped them into the sea under heavy security cover. From another boat nearby, soldiers blasted the cylinders floating on the water with cannons. The harmful chemical gases would have surely affected marine life in the area. Where human life has no value, why would a thought be spared for marine life?

All countries manufacturing chemical and biological weapons have done the same. The oceans have gulped down so much poison that if they are churned today, not only Shiva, all the gods will turn black and blue! At that time, it was thought that the chemicals would vanish into the unfathomable depths, and the salinity of sea water would render the poisons ineffective. But nothing like that happened.

Based on the history of Earth, there are hills and valleys in oceans, and vast storehouses of poisonous gases are hiding in their caverns and crevices. Most of these chemicals are denser than water and hence lie spread out on the ocean floor; mustard gas is one such chemical. Earthquakes keep happening under the ocean's surface, stirring up this chemical cocktail. They are thrown out on the shores along with waves and caught in fishing nets.

In 1946, within a year of the end of the Second World War, hundreds of such bombs were found in the Gulf of Mexico and the seas around Italy. It has been reported how a number of cans of mustard gas were found on the shores of Australia in January 1970, with investigations looking for a culprit. A report titled 'Chemical Munitions Sea Dumping Off Australia' prepared by Australian government Department Of Defence gives elaborate information in this regard. The same was found to be true with mustard gas cans drowned in the Asian seas. Six years later, such substances were found in the Hawaiian Islands while mining for sand. Even in 2004, such weapons were found in creeks close to New Jersey. These are instances that have been recorded. It is worth remembering that all these countries are wealthy and developed, where human life is valued. But in the poorer Asian and African countries, such accidents would have surely gone unnoticed.

But such carelessness is of course not acceptable in the US, where there is great awareness about personal health. The US constituted a Congress committee of experts to study the weapons drowned in the oceans. It looked into all aspects of disposal of chemical weapons in general and particularly in the ocean. Parallelly, the US's security team of experts began gathering information. In the report submitted to Congress in 2001, one point came out clearly: America had drowned chemical and biological weapons at a scale much larger than was known. The committee accepted this right in the beginning of the probe and reported seventy-four such instances of drowning weapons. Of these, in thirty-two instances, weapons had been dumped in the seas bordering the US itself. The remaining forty-two were put into foreign seas. The report accepted that the US had dumped these contaminants in the courtyards of other countries in large proportions.

The US took this route for the first time in 1918, during the First World War, throwing chemicals into the Atlantic Ocean between England and America. It lost a lot of respect because it had committed the same crime in the Pacific Ocean, Gulf of Mexico, Indian Ocean, near the Hawaiian Islands and also in the Mississippi River!

What was drowned?

Thousands of mustard gas bombs and mustard gas stores, hydrogen cyanide cylinders, millions of drums full of arsenic, 375 tons of tear gas, 46,000 fumigation bombs, 190 tons of Lewisite and lakhs of phosgene bombs. As if this wasn't enough, radioactive waste weighing 4,21,757 pounds was dumped as well. All these substances must be somewhere in the depths of the Atlantic Ocean even today. Cleaning this mess is a technical challenge and there are chances of accidents that can be lethal. This too has been mentioned in the report.

These instances increased so much that in 1972, the US Congress passed the Ocean Dumping Ban Act. Towards the end of 1969, President Richard Nixon declared a complete ban on chemical weapons in the US. As a result of that and an increase in protests in the US, corrective measures had to be taken. Owing to this, America's environment preservation machinery became more powerful and instances of dumping hazardous chemical weapons developed in the US labs too reduced considerably.

Apart from evil deeds, other countries have followed the US's good deeds as well. England too started similar clean-up campaigns in the country. In 2005, London's Imperial College conducted a survey and found that the chemical weapons dumped in seas not as deep as the Baltic Sea could prove hazardous even today. Following the survey, England too took up the task of cleaning the ocean. But this was a shallow exercise because it knew that this was an impossible and expensive exercise. In 2006, the US presented its defence budget that gave an estimate about the expenses involved in cleaning up the oceans. The US alone would have to spend $34,000 million. It must have concluded that there was no point in spending so much on what had already happened; it would be wiser to focus on new research initiatives and innovations.

That is how fresh research on chemical and biological weapons started. It is true that not all of this research was harmful. Some of it

was also for the benefit of health and wellness. But the concern that
it was being used against mankind worried experts all over the world.
The truth about the history of human progress is that with one step
taken in the direction of development, we also move four backwards.

For instance, take the field of genetic engineering. Our genes
determine our skin colour, height, eye colour, hair texture and so on.
Genetic engineering has created possibilities for changing all this.
Using this technology, we can change our physical attributes. Genetic
engineering coupled with microbiological research is causing radical
changes in our lives, some of which are certainly for the better. For
example, these days crops do not fall prey to pest infestation like
before. Pomegranate seeds are redder, and several fruits are available
all year round. It is possible that owing to such research, we might
get seedless custard apples in the near future or longer and longer
cotton threads.[109]

But the concerns revolve around the problems that can be caused
by the abnormal and perverse use of this technology. The unrestricted
use of microbiology and genetic engineering is also raising questions
about ethics, morals and social issues. For example, seeds immune
to disease are being created and at the same time microorganisms
resistant to pesticides have developed. If the direction of this
development changes, it will be like the hunter being hunted. If
someone develops a super potent microbe in the lab using these
modern techniques and attacks enemy countries with them, the
results can be catastrophic.

Knowing that such things are possible, the chief of the science
and ethics department of the Medical Society of United Kingdom
on Science, Dr Wayne Nathanson, warned that gene therapy might
possibly be turned into gene weapons which could potentially be

---

109 Jan van Aken and Edward Hammond, *Genetic Engineering and
Biological Weapons*.

used to target particular genes possessed by certain groups of people. These need not be delivered using existing forms of warfare like gases or aerosols, but could also be added to water supplies or spread through crops.

The reality of his warning came true within a year's time. The *London Times* reported in detail on 15 November 1998 that Israel had made biological weapons to be used against Palestinians which had the potential to destroy future generations. Once such explosive news is published, others try to follow it up with more details. The *Sunday Times* did exactly that. At that time, Israel did not affirm the news, but neither did they refute it. They just said they had enough weapons to shock the strongest of countries. This caused further doubts to be raised. The suspicions became stronger because South Africa was a partner of Israel in these experiments. It is a well-known fact that the erstwhile Apartheid regime of South Africa had tried to create biological/genetic weapons to annihilate black Africans. Israel joined South Africa and the dangerous partnership would have hurt both parties equally.[110]

It is not like these were the only two countries involved in such activities. The US and Russia too weren't far behind. The US reported to have made plague-causing bacteria more resistant, while Russia is alleged to have gone a step ahead and changed the genes of the anthrax-causing bacteria. Russian scientists are believed to have planted a new virus into the genes of the anthrax-causing bacteria— *Bacillus anthracis*. The new third-generation virus developed as a result made the anthrax microbe so miniscule that it went beyond any preventive medicine. Though its size became smaller, its contagious effects didn't reduce. If an anthrax epidemic had spread because of this microbe, it would have been extremely difficult to

---

110 Mahnaimi, Uzi and Marie Colvin, 'Israel Planning "Ethnic" Bomb as Saddam Caves in,' *Sunday Times*, 15 November 1998.

control. No preventive medicine or antibiotic would have worked. Fortunately, this strain of anthrax is still confined to the laboratories and hasn't been used.

But the very existence of such weapons is like a sword hanging over our heads. They could come out of labs for reasons like political disagreements, tensions caused due to trade policies, or the emergence of some rabid ruler.

This is not the only microbe confined to a lab. There are some important microbes leading protected lives within American and Russian laboratories. It has been more than two decades since smallpox has been eradicated from the world. It doesn't exist anywhere, other than the US and Russia. The smallpox virus is being preserved in laboratories in these two countries. It is kept under stringent security and protected like a national treasure.

We may feel that these microbes cannot escape easily because of how they are stored. This false sense of security could prove short-lived because the technology for developing them artificially has emerged. In 2002, the journal *Science* created a storm by reporting in detail the development of the polio virus by scientists at New York University. They had used some commonly available DNA and artificial chemicals to produce it. They mentioned that several viruses with simple DNA strands could now be created artificially in labs—all of them disease-causing viruses. The Ebola and Marburg viruses and the Venezuelan encephalitis diseases can henceforth be artificially created. The next shocking news is that some members of the Aum cult in Japan had actually taken up such experiments, but severe crackdowns meant they couldn't continue.

All this means that we no longer need one species to create another. They can be mass produced like matchsticks in a factory. We had heard news of such experiments in May 2010, such as the Human Genome Project. There is another aspect to the success of this project. Till then there was governmental control over such experiments and they took place only in government labs. But what happened in May 2010 was in laboratories belonging to private companies. Synthetic Genomes is the first company in this sector. It is considered the Microsoft of the biotechnology sector, and its founder Dr John Craig Venter is seen as the Bill Gates of this field. Dr Venter and his company created history on 20 May 2010.[111]

Dr Venter is considered a rebel in his field. In early 2000, he procured a patent for a human gene, which was unheard of till then—totally different from patents for product, innovations or design. Everyone including the US President was shocked because it hadn't struck anyone till then that something like this was possible. In 2007, the reputed and respected journal *New Scientist* published an interview with Dr Venter. The man was a visionary, and he said, 'I am certain that I will be able to produce synthetic cells in my laboratory.' He proved it within three years and declared his success on 20 May 2010. People find it difficult to decide where to place this feat. Should they praise it as a scientific achievement or focus on the scary consequences of what he had accomplished?

In short, what Dr Venter had done was create a synthetic cell. He took a synthetic bacterial genome constructed from chemicals in the laboratory and 'booted it up' by inserting it into a living single-celled bacterium. The cell replicated itself into a colony of organisms containing only the synthetic DNA.

In 2008, Venter and his collaborator Hamilton Smith created the first synthetic bacterial genome by building a modified version of M. genitalium's DNA. Then, in 2010, they made the first self-replicating synthetic organism, manufacturing a version of M. mycoides' genome and then transplanting it into a different mycoplasma species. The synthetic genome took over the cell, replacing the native operating

---

111   Ian Sample, 'Craig Venter Creates Synthetic Life Form', *The Guardian*, 20 May 2010.

system with a human-made version. The synthetic M. mycoides genome was mostly identical to the natural version, save for a few genetic watermarks.[112]

New Scientist wrote while reporting this experiment, 'What Dr Venter has done can be achieved with other cells as well. When that happens, it will become possible to create or fuse genes and cells of our choice in the laboratory. This would open doors to newer areas in biotechnology and genetic engineering. This is the constructive side of science and poses no concerns, but what is worrisome is the potential destructive side to it.'

Elizabeth Pennisi wrote a commentary in the same issue of *Science* on Dr Venter's work. She cited anthropologist Paul Rabinow and Massachusetts Institute of Technology sociologist Kenneth Oye. According to Rabinow, 'We need to understand our concept of ethical and unethical practices in a newer light following the success of the Human Genome Project.' Oye said, 'It is our misfortune that there is a huge possibility of this new research being misused. That is why it is imperative for the law makers of the world to come together as soon as possible and decide how and where to use this new scientific development. It is a need of the hour.'

When there are so many new developments taking place in this field in England and the US, why should we in India create a big deal of the matter? There may not have been much fundamental research in this field in India, but we are head-to-head with developed nations in terms of its commercialization. We have just opened up this field to private companies. A large company known more for its political clout than its technical capabilities has set up a sister concern for the manufacture of biological products and has already started work.

---

112 Wired, 'The Mystery of the Minimal Cell, Craig Venter's New Synthetic Life Form', 26 March 2016.

We Indians are anyway known to first start playing the game and deciding the rules later! For instance, we have allowed private companies into the aviation sector and are now discussing ways to monitor and check their functioning. We have done the same in telecommunication and insurance. So it comes as no surprise that it's the same with biotechnology. This is how consistency is maintained even in mismanagement!

A lot of progress has been made in the applications of stem cells in private hospitals and pharmaceutical companies.[113] On the surface, stem cells are no different from other cells, but they have some distinctive abilities. Stem cells are the body's raw materials—cells from which all other cells with specialized functions are generated. Under the right conditions in the body or a lab, stem cells divide to form more cells called daughter cells. Moreover, they have no specific individual characteristics. For example, some cells are specifically born as cardiac or brain cells and cannot be used in other organs, whereas stem cells are different. They are non-specific, and the daughter cells either become new stem cells (self-renewal) or become specialized cells (differentiation) with a more specific function, such as blood cells, brain cells, heart muscle cells or bone cells. No other cell in the body has the natural ability to generate new cell types.

Almost 200 types of cells needed in the body can be produced from stem cells. Let's say someone's pancreas is damaged; stem cells can be incorporated into the damaged pancreas and new pancreatic cells regenerated. This is called stem cell therapy. There are several specialized stem cells. Some are present only when the foetus is in the womb (embryonic stem cells). There are some which die the moment the placenta separates. That is why these stem cells can be collected during pregnancy and stored for future use. There is a

---

113 'Stem Cells: What They Are and What They Do', Mayo Clinic.

laboratory in Delhi that is providing this service, which is in great demand. People store their embryonic stem cells in this laboratory the way they store jewellery in bank lockers! Though stem cell lockers cost Rs 75,000 as a one-time payment, there is a long waiting list.

Realizing that stem cells would be the cure of choice in the days to come, several private hospitals have made huge investments in this area. Around Rs 1,44,000 crore or $3,000 million was spent on stem cell therapy in 2009. Experts estimate that the figure would have risen to $16,000 million or Rs 4,60,800 crore by 2015. The Indian government has taken cognizance of the rapid growth in stem cell therapy and the biotechnology department has taken up research on stem cells in eighteen important laboratories. The government has set up an institution called Institute for Stem Cell Biology and Regenerative Medicine with its headquarters in Bangalore. It was given a grant of Rs 300 crore in 2010.

The same America which was at the forefront of stem cell research stopped all work in this area during the term of George W. Bush. Even Christian religious heads opposed this research. Both Bush and the Church were against abortions and they used the same reasons to oppose stem cell research. Both felt it was akin to interfering and playing with nature. Barack Obama, Bush's successor, overturned the prohibitory orders and reinstated stem cell research. Given this background, it is indeed laudable that the Indian government has been giving an impetus for stem cell research from day one.

While on one side there are so many constructive developments, on the other there are people who are trying hard to block such efforts. In June 2010, the American security agencies hinted at the possible risk, saying, 'Future biological wars would be fought with bacteria.' Biological weapons so far have needed some carrier or instrument like a spray, but those made with bacteria can be used very easily by mixing with air or water. This is not an empty threat because Australian and American scientists have shown that it is possible to spread disease using bacteria. The disease's name is Melioidosis, caused by the bacterium Burkholderia pseudomallei. It can easily spread through water and air. Melioidosis can attack the lungs and cause a range of conditions from mild bronchitis to severe pneumonia. As a result, patients may also experience fever, headache, loss of appetite (anorexia), cough, shortness of breath, chest pain and general muscle soreness. Incidences of this disease have been reported in Asia[114] and several African countries.

That is how the genes have been flowing. We need to think of ways to stem the flow right away.

---

114 P.R. Mohapatra and B. Mishra, 'Burden of Melioidosis in India and South Asia: Challenges and Ways Forward', *The Lancet*, 5 May 2022, https://www.thelancet.com/journals/lansea/article/PIIS2772-3682(22)00004-X/fulltext

Afterword

Let Everything Be Free from Illness

THE appearance of the bird flu and swine flu epidemics helped the inconsequential pharmaceutical company Gilead Life Sciences blossom into a global giant in no time. The person who enjoyed the fruits of this rise the most was none other than the chairman of the company, Donald Rumsfeld.

Fortune magazine published that Rumsfeld held the reins of the company from 1997 to 2001. The shake-up of the national health services around the same time created such a massive demand for the company's sole product that its share prices hit the roof. Rumsfeld was clever enough to realize that it was the right time to make the best of the opportunity. He sold a large percentage of his shares in the company. He saw his already massive net worth of a billion dollars swell by a few millions overnight. Around $50 million went into Rumsfeld's bank account through the sale of shares of just one company. As per reports, he still owns Gilead shares worth at least

$15 million. Several newspapers have reported the kind of profits he made as a result of the bird flu epidemic.[115]

Meanwhile, Gilead Life Sciences sold the licence for the manufacture of Tamiflu to Swiss pharmaceutical giant Roche. But Bush and Rumsfeld being in power and the spread of the bird flu and swine flu epidemics coincided, and the global demand for Tamiflu increased by around 500 per cent. Although Gilead had sold the manufacturing licence, it still held the patent for Tamiflu. Gilead informed Roche that they could not manufacture the drug any longer. But Roche had not got into the pharmaceutical business for charity, and it filed a suit against the American company. Roche claimed that Gilead Life Sciences had breached its own agreement solely for commercial profits. The case was finally closed in 2005.[116] According to the settlement, Roche would get a royalty of 4 per cent of the price of every Tamiflu tablet sold anywhere in the world. Gilead receives a royalty from Roche equalling about 10 per cent of sales.

In 2009, the Maharashtra state government alone ordered 20 million Tamiflu tablets supposedly to ensure our health and safety. It is nobody's guess whether it was our health that improved or the financial health of Gilead. Another event worth mentioning is that US President George W. Bush too accumulated Tamiflu stock worth $20 million. The similarity between the Maharashtra government and Bush ends there.

Later, Bush ordered a further $75 million worth of Tamiflu stock. Owing to all these efforts, Tamiflu alone reported to have earned $250 million in 2004, which rose to $1 billion in 2005. Swine flu

---

115 'Rumsfeld to Avoid Bird-Flu Drug Issues', *The New York Times*, 28 October 2005, https://www.nytimes.com/2005/10/28/politics/rumsfeld-to-avoid-birdflu-drug-issues.html

116 'Gilead and Roche End Tamiflu(R) Dispute', Gilead.com, 16 November 2005.

made its appearance next, and everyone began consuming Tamiflu left right and centre. Gilead made massive profits around that time!

It is not as if such things were happening for the first time. In 1971, the US was accused of deliberately spreading bird flu during its conflict with Fidel Castro's communist Cuba.[117] Drums full of bird flu germs were shipped from the CIA's secret centres in the Panama Canal region, it was reported. The Cuban government was forced to kill about half a million pigs due to the flu epidemic. The US had hoped that this would cause a food shortage in Cuba and the Cubans would revolt against Castro. But despite America's dirty tricks, Castro was still going strong even in 2010. He passed away in 2016.

There was widespread criticism about what happened in Cuba. Arthur M. Silverstein, professor at Johns Hopkins University, wrote about this in chilling detail in his bestselling book Pure Politics and Impure Science: The Swine Flu Affair. According to the book, much before Bush, former US President Gerald Ford played a major role in spreading bird flu. A similar hullabaloo had been created about a bird flu epidemic in 1975–76. With an eye on winning the following election on his own strength and to show his concern for public health and safety, Ford devised an ambitious plan of vaccinating 220 million American citizens against bird flu at a cost of $135 million. These unnecessary vaccinations resulted in hundreds of recipients being paralysed. Consequently, the vaccination programme had to be aborted, Ford lost the elections and Jimmy Carter became President of America.

The question is, was the wave of swine flu that occurred recently man-made?

It is difficult to give a definite answer, but going by history, we cannot say for certain whether such issues were restricted to swine flu

---

117 *San Francisco Chronicle*, 'CIA Link to Cuban Pig Virus Reported', 10 January 1977.

and bird flu. It is true that the people of less developed countries have been used as guinea pigs for drug trials deliberately or inadvertently. It is the fate of small fish to satiate the hunger of the big ones. That is the law of the jungle.

Are humans too living by the laws of the jungle, even in these modern times? Some of us should try to find the answer to this question and gather the courage to reveal it to the world.

If not, shut this book and don't allow the mind to get agitated.

Just close your eyes and lie silently and helplessly!

Bibliography

Thomas J. Johnson, 'A History of Biological Warfare from 300 BCE to the Present', Web Health Search, https://www.webhealthsearch.com/infections/biological-warfare/

C. Hilmas, Jeffrey Smart and Benjamin Hill, 'Chapter 2', *History of Chemical and Biological Warfare: An American Perspective*, Homeland Security Digital Library, pp, 1–3.

Robert Graves, *The Greek Myths: The Complete and Definitive Edition*, Viking, 2018.

'St. Joan of Arc', *Catholic Encyclopedia*.

Edward Jenner (1749–1823), https://www.bbc.co.uk/history/historic_figures/jenner_edward.shtml

Stefan Riedel, 'Edward Jenner and the History of Smallpox and Vaccination', Proceedings (Baylor University. Medical Center), 2005, https://www.ncbi.nlm.nih.gov/pmc/articles/PMC1200696/

Robert Harris and Jeremy Paxman, *A Higher Form of Killing: The Secret History of Chemical and Biological Warfare*, Random House, 2002, pp. 3–7.

William D. James, Timothy G. Berger and Dirk M. Elston, *Andrews' Diseases of the Skin: Clinical Dermatology*, Elsevier, Eleventh edition, 2011.

Robert Koenig, *The Fourth Horseman: One Man's Mission to Wage the Great War in America*, PublicAffairs, 2007.

Jeanne Guillemin, *Biological Weapons: From the Invention of State-Sponsored Programs to Contemporary Bioterrorism*, Columbia University Press, 2006.

David Nicolle and Raffaele Ruggeri, *The Italian Invasion of Abyssinia 1935-36*, Osprey Publishing, 2012.

A.J. Barker, *The Rape of Ethiopia 1936*, Ballantine Books, 1971.

BBC, 'China and Japan: Rival Giants and Rape of Nanjing', 17 June 2011.

Marvin Tokayer and Mary Swartz, *The Fugu Plan: The Untold Story of the Japanese and the Jews during World War II*, Gefen Publishing House, 2004.

John M. Jennings, *The Opium Empire: Japanese Imperialism and Drug Trafficking in Asia, 1895–1945*, Praeger Publishers, 1997.

Herbert P. Bix, *Hirohito and the Making of Modern Japan*, Harper Perennial, 2001.

Yuki Tanaka, *Hidden Horrors: Japanese War Crimes in World War II*, Rowman & Littlefield, 2017.

Daniel Barenblatt, *A Plague Upon Humanity: The Secret Genocide of Axis Japan's Germ Warfare Operation*, HarperCollins Publishers, 2004.

Bernard Wasserstein, Secret War in Shanghai: An Untold Story of Espionage, Intrigue, and Treason in World War II, , Houghton Mifflin, 1999.

Albert Speer, *Inside the Third Reich*, Simon & Schuster, 1997.

Giles Milton, 'Winston Churchill's Shocking Use of Chemical Weapons', *The Guardian*, 1 September 2013, https://www.theguardian.com/world/shortcuts/2013/sep/01/winston-churchill-shocking-use-chemical-weapons#:~:text=As%20

a%20long%2Dterm%20advocate,the%20use%20of%20
chemical%20weapons

W. Seth Carus, 'A Short History of Biological Warfare: From Pre-History to the 21st Century', Center for the Study of Weapons of Mass Destruction Occasional Paper, No. 12, National Defense University Press, August 2017, https://ndupress.ndu.edu/Portals/68/Documents/occasional/cswmd/CSWMD_OccasionalPaper-12.pdf

Ken Alibek, *Biohazard: The Chilling True Story of the Largest Covert Biological Weapons Program in the World--Told from Inside by the Man Who Ran It*, Delta, 2000.

Mark Weber, 'Secrets of the Soviet Disease Warfare Program: Were Biological Weapons Used against Germans at Stalingrad?', *The Journal of Historical Review*, Vol. 18, No. 2, March/April 1999.

Thaddeus Wittlin, *Commissar: The Life and Death of Lavrenty Pavlovich Beria*, Angus & Robertson, 1973.

David Willman, 'Selling the Threat of Bioterrorism', *Los Angeles Times*, 1 July 2007, https://www.latimes.com/archives/la-xpm-2007-jul-01-na-alibek1-story.html

Ed Regis, *The Biology of Doom: The History of America's Secret Germ Warfare Project*, Holt, 2000.

'Cheney & Rumsfeld Linked Murder of CIA Scientist', News at freedomarchives.org, 25 June 2004.

'Battlefield: Vietnam', PBS, www.pbs.org/battlefieldvietnam/timeline

'The Virtual Vietnam Archive', Texas Tech University, https://www.vietnam.ttu.edu/virtualarchive/

'Chemical Warfare: Use of Herbicides during the Vietnam War', https://science.jrank.org/pages/1391/Chemical-Warfare-Use-herbicides-during-Vietnam-War.html

'Vietnam War U.S. Military Fatal Casualty Statistics', Military Records, National Archives, https://www.archives.gov/research/military/vietnam-war/casualty-statistics

'Munitions', Military, GlobalSecurity.org, www.globalsecurity.org/military/systems/munitions

Foreign Relations of the United States, 1969-1976, Volume E-2, Documents on Arms Control and Nonproliferation, 1969-1972.

Mike Thomson, 'Pont-Saint-Esprit poisoning: Did the CIA spread LSD?', BBC News, 23 August 2010, https://www.bbc.com/news/world-10996838

BBC, 'MK Ultra: The Secrets of the CIA's Mind-Control Programme', 29 March 2022, https://www.historyextra.com/period/20th-century/mk-ultra-secrets-cia-mind-control-programme-central-intelligance-agency-brainwashing/

US Congressional Record: 20 September 2002 (Senate).

Julian Borger, 'Rumsfeld "Offered Help to Saddam"', *The Guardian*, 31 December 2002, https://www.theguardian.com/world/2002/dec/31/iraq.politics

Adam Jones, ed., *Gendercide and Genocide*, Vanderbilt University Press, 2004.

Adam Jones, ed., *Genocide, War Crimes and the West: History and Complicity*, Zed Books, 2004.

Independent, 'Chemical Ali: The End of an Overlord', 25 June 2007.

Susan Webb, 'Why the U.S. concealed its chemical weapons role in Iraq', PeoplesWorld.org, , 20 October 2014, https://www.peoplesworld.org/article/why-the-u-s-concealed-its-chemical-weapons-role-in-iraq/

Judith Miller, Stephen Engelberg and William Broad, *Germs: Biological Weapons and America's Secret War*, Simon & Schuster, 2002.

Stephen M. Walt, 'WikiLeaks, April Glaspie, and Saddam Hussein', *Foreign Policy*, 9 January 2011, https://foreignpolicy.com/2011/01/09/wikileaks-april-glaspie-and-saddam-hussein/

Phillip Knightley, 'The Disinformation Campaign', *The Guardian*, 4 October 2001, https://www.theguardian.com/education/2001/oct/04/socialsciences.highereducation

Steve Coll, *The Bin Ladens: An Arabian Family in the American Century*, Penguin Books, 2009.

Adam Robinson, *Bin Laden: Behind the Mask of the Terrorist*, Mainstream Publishing, 2001.

Frances M. Murphy, 'Gulf War Syndrome', *British Medical Journal*, 1999, https://www.ncbi.nlm.nih.gov/pmc/articles/PMC1114762/

John King, 'Arming Iraq: A Chronology of US Involvement', Iran Chamber Society, March 2003, https://www.iranchamber.com/history/articles/arming_iraq.php

Murray S. Waas and Craig Unger, 'In the Loop: Bush's Secret Mission', *The New Yorker*, 25 October 1992, https://www.newyorker.com/magazine/1992/11/02/in-the-loop-bushs-secret-mission

Danylo Chaykovsky, 'Stepan Bandera, His Life and Struggle', http://exlibris.org.ua/murders/r04.html

Stephen Adams, 'Revealed: Sex Hormone Plan to Feminise Hitler', *The Telegraph*, 14 August 2011, https://www.telegraph.co.uk/news/8701024/Revealed-sex-hormone-plan-to-feminise-Hitler.html#:~:text=Agents%20planned%20to%20smuggle%20doses,Ford%2C%20who%20discovered%20the%20plot

Jasmine Garsd, 'Long Before Facebook, The KGB Spread Fake News About AIDS', NPR.org, 22 August 2018, https://www.npr.org/2018/08/22/640883503/long-before-facebook-the-kgb-spread-fake-news-about-aids

Jan van Aken and Edward Hammond, 'Genetic Engineering and Biological Weapons', *Embo Reports*, June 2003, https://www.ncbi.nlm.nih.gov/pmc/articles/PMC1326447/

Daniel Schorn, 'Who Killed Alexander Litvinenko?', CBS, 5 January 2007, https://www.cbsnews.com/news/who-killed-alexander-litvinenko/

Zeyno Baran, S. Frederick Starr and Svante E. Cornell, 'Islamic Radicalism in Central Asia and the Caucasus', Central Asia-Caucasus Institute and Silk Road Studies Program, July 2006, https://www.silkroadstudies.org/resources/

pdf/SilkRoadPapers/2006_07_SRP_BaranStarrCornell_
Radicalism.pdf

Gordon Thomas and David Dastych, 'Dysfunctions: Bio-Roulette',
Canada Free Press, 17 October 2005, https://canadafreepress.
com/2005/dastych101705.htm

Catherine Collins, 'Ma Anand Sheela: Media Power through
Radical Discourses', in Andrew King (ed.), *Postmodern Political
Communication: The Fringe Challenges the Center*, Praeger
Publishers, 1992.

Sven Davisson, 'The Rise & Fall of Rajneeshpuram', Archives of
Ashé Journal, Vol 2, Issue 2, 2003, published on 15 March
2015, https://ashejournal.com/2015/03/15/ashe-journal-vol-2-
issue-2-2003/

James S. Gordon, *The Golden Guru: The Strange Journey of Bhagwan
Shree Rajneesh*, Stephen Greene Pr, 1987.

OregonLive, '25 Years after Rajneeshee Commune Collapsed, Truth
Spills Out', 5 February 2019, https://www.oregonlive.com/
rajneesh/2011/04/part_one_it_was_worse_than_we.html

David M. Bearden, 'US Disposal of Chemical Weapons in the Ocean:
Background and Issues for Congress', Library of Congress
Washington DC Congressional Research Service, 13 July 2006,
https://apps.dtic.mil/sti/citations/ADA462443

Mahnaimi, Uzi and Marie Colvin, 'Israel Planning "Ethnic" Bomb
as Saddam Caves In', *Sunday Times*, 15 November 1998.

Ian Sample, 'Craig Venter Creates Synthetic Life Form', *The
Guardian*, 20 May 2010, https://www.theguardian.com/
science/2010/may/20/craig-venter-synthetic-life-form

Wired, 'The Mystery of the Minimal Cell, Craig Venter's New
Synthetic Life Form', 26 March 2016, https://www.wired.
com/2016/03/mystery-minimal-cell-craig-venters-new-
synthetic-life-form/

'Stem Cells: What They Are and What They Do', Mayo Clinic,
https://www.mayoclinic.org/tests-procedures/bone-marrow-
transplant/in-depth/stem-cells/art-20048117

P.R. Mohapatra and B. Mishra, 'Burden of Melioidosis in India and South Asia: Challenges and Ways Forward', *The Lancet*, 5 May 2022, https://www.thelancet.com/journals/lansea/article/PIIS2772-3682(22)00004-X/fulltext

'Rumsfeld to Avoid Bird-Flu Drug Issues', *The New York Times*, 28 October 2005, https://www.nytimes.com/2005/10/28/politics/rumsfeld-to-avoid-birdflu-drug-issues.html

'Gilead and Roche End Tamiflu(R) Dispute; Expanded Collaboration Includes Gilead Role in Oversight of Manufacturing and Commercialization', Gilead.com, 16 November 2005, https://www.gilead.com/news-and-press/press-room/press-releases/2005/11/gilead-and-roche-end-tamiflur-dispute-expanded-collaboration-includes-gilead-role-in-oversight-of-manufacturing-and-commercialization

San Francisco Chronicle, 'CIA Link to Cuban Pig Virus Reported', 10 January 1977.

Index

Acknowledgements

This book wouldn't have been in English but for HarperCollins *Publishers* India. I am thankful to them for having chosen this for translation and then for assigning it to three excellent editors— Siddhesh Inamdar, Suchismita Ukil and Ujjaini Dasgupta. Originally published in Marathi as *Yuddha Jivanche*, it was Ms Subha Pande whose tireless efforts resulted in its English translation. A big thank you to her.

The cover wonderfully captures the essence of the book. I cannot thank Alan Hebel and Ian Koviak of theBookdesigners enough for such a striking and creative cover design.

About the Author

Girish Kuber is the editor of the Marathi daily *Loksatta* of the Indian Express Group. He is the author of *The Tatas: How a Family Built a Business and a Nation* and *Renaissance State: The Unwritten Story of the Making of Maharashtra*. He has written six books in Marathi and lives in Mumbai.

Subha Pande is a multilingual translator and has translated Kaajal Oza Vaidya's *Krishnayan* into English (*Eka*, 2021), and Kavita Kané's *Sita's Sister* and *The Fisher Queen's Dynasty* into Hindi. She has also translated six novellas and a short-story collection by Sivasankari into English. Pande is a certified yoga instructor and lives in Vadodara with her writer husband Vikrant Pande.

30 Years *of*

HarperCollins *Publishers* India

At HarperCollins, we believe in telling the best stories and finding the widest possible readership for our books in every format possible. We started publishing 30 years ago; a great deal has changed since then, but what has remained constant is the passion with which our authors write their books, the love with which readers receive them, and the sheer joy and excitement that we as publishers feel in being a part of the publishing process.

Over the years, we've had the pleasure of publishing some of the finest writing from the subcontinent and around the world, and some of the biggest bestsellers in India's publishing history. Our books and authors have won a phenomenal range of awards, and we ourselves have been named Publisher of the Year the greatest number of times. But nothing has meant more to us than the fact that millions of people have read the books we published, and somewhere, a book of ours might have made a difference.

As we step into our fourth decade, we go back to that one word – a word which has been a driving force for us all these years.

Read.

Harper
Collins

HARPER
PERENNIAL

HARPER
BUSINESS

HARPER
BLACK

हार्पर
हिन्दी

HarperCollins
Children'sBooks

HARPER
DESIGN

HARPER
VANTAGE

Harper
Sport